What readers are saying about *The Whole You* ...

"Tanis is a masterful teacher, healer and spiritual leader who presents concepts with clarity and simple truth. This book invites the reader on an inspired evolutionary journey that will enrich their whole being—mind, body and spirit."
　Dr. Sharon Goodyear-Johnston

"This book is a 'must read' for anyone interested in true healing or wanting to understand who they are beyond the physical realm. Tanis takes you on a marvelous journey through the human energy fields and describes in detail how and why we become the individuals we are. You will feel 'enlightened' as you take this *'fantastic voyage'* into spirit!"
　Wendy Robertson

"This is the book I've been waiting for-something to expand upon the complex concepts of energy healing and to be a companion on my learning journey."
　Heather Cain

"If you want to heal, transform and find out who you truly are ... read this book and Tanis will show you the way!"
　Jennifer Williams

"This is the only book I'm aware of that brings your Higher Self into active practice."
　Jacqueline Bergeron

"Tanis' work provides a completely joyful opportunity to look into the window of your soul."
  Madeleine Chevrier

"This is the book I've been waiting for. Read it and you'll know why!"
  Elizabeth Skronski

THE WHOLE YOU

THE WHOLE YOU

HEALING AND TRANSFORMATION THROUGH ENERGY AWARENESS

Tanis Day PhD

iUniverse, Inc.
New York Lincoln Shanghai

THE WHOLE YOU
HEALING AND TRANSFORMATION THROUGH ENERGY AWARENESS

Copyright © 2008 by Tanis Day

All rights reserved. No part of this book may be used or reproduced by any means, graphic, electronic, or mechanical, including photocopying, recording, taping or by any information storage retrieval system without the written permission of the publisher except in the case of brief quotations embodied in critical articles and reviews.

iUniverse books may be ordered through booksellers or by contacting:

iUniverse
2021 Pine Lake Road, Suite 100
Lincoln, NE 68512
www.iuniverse.com
1-800-Authors (1-800-288-4677)

Because of the dynamic nature of the Internet, any Web addresses or links contained in this book may have changed since publication and may no longer be valid.

The views expressed in this work are solely those of the author and do not necessarily reflect the views of the publisher, and the publisher hereby disclaims any responsibility for them.

ISBN: 978-0-595-45940-7 (pbk)
ISBN: 978-0-595-70993-9 (cloth)
ISBN: 978-0-595-90240-8 (ebk)

Printed in the United States of America

To all my client-student-friends,
who made this work possible.

Table of Contents

What readers are saying about *The Whole You* i

Foreword xv

Introduction: The Nonphysical World xxi

1. Becoming Conscious of Consciousness 1
    Consciousness as Raw Material 2
    Making Things Matter 4
    The Power of Choice 5
    Practical Exercises 7
        Moving your Point of Awareness 7
        Witnessing your Energetic Reactions 8
        'Coming In' from the Mental Body 9

2. Overview of the Human Energy Fields 13
    Perceiving the Energy Fields 13
    The Layers of Dimensions 17
    The Chakra System 20
    Chakras Come in Sets of Three 21
    The Seven Body Chakras 23

3. The Personality: This Lifetime's Experience 29
    The Unaware Personality 29

Bringing Awareness to the Personality 34
The Emotional Body 35
Practical Exercises 39
    Exploring your Emotional Body 39
    Feeling Emotions 41
The Mental Body 41
Practical Exercises 47
    Exploring Your Mental Body 47
    Finding Memories 47
How the Emotional and Mental Bodies Work Together 51
Practical Exercises 54
    Exploring the Mental-Emotional Interaction 54

4. Don't Believe Your Beliefs 56
Illusion and Projection 59
Why we Believe our Beliefs 62

5. The Soul Level: Past Lives and the Collective Unconscious 68
Perceiving the Soul Field 71
Reincarnation and the Etheric Template 72
Identical Twins 76
Healing with the Etheric Template 78
Karma 80
Soul Patterns 82
Spiritual Contracts 83
Why We Forget 84
Practical Exercises 87
    Exploring the Soul Field 87

6. The Higher Dimensions 89
The Monad 92
The Master Level 96
The Co-Creative Dimension 98

Unified Consciousness...99
Practical Exercises 101
    Exploring the Higher Dimensions................................101

7. Making Use of Guidance...103
Receiving Input 106
Asking Questions 110
Interpreting Accurately..112

8. Demystifying the Dark 119
Personal Dark...121
Dark Consciousness...123
The Human-Dark Relationship 127
The Solution...128
Practical Exercises 129
    Recognizing Dark Consciousness...............................129
    Breaking Contracts with the Dark 130

9. Putting it all Together—Self-Realization 132
Self-Realization through Self-Awareness 133
Noticing..134
Exploring..139
Experimenting...141

10. Putting it All Together—Healing................................145
Healing when Triggered...146
Healing Specific Topics...148
Healing as a Tune-Up...151
Physical Healing..152
Cross-Fertilization in Healing 153

11. Putting it all Together—Spiritual Enlightenment.......155
The Evolving Mind 158

Table of Contents

The Energy Fields as a Map to Enlightenment 162
The Soul Merge 165
The Monadic Merge 167
The Higher Merges 169
Practical Exercises 171
    Assuming Beliefs are not True *171*
    What did I learn today? *171*
    Dissolving Identity *171*
    Exploring the Higher Chakras *172*

Endnotes 175

List of Figures

Figure 1—Layers of the Human Energy Fields 16

Figure 2—Schematic Impression of the Chakra System 22

Figure 3—The Emotional Body 36

Figure 4—The Mental Body 43

Figure 5—The Soul Field 70

Figure 6—The Monadic Field or the Higher Self 94

Foreword

As a child I knew I wanted to be a spiritual teacher. I felt called to become a minister, but in the early 1960's this was too radical an idea. I was told I couldn't be a minister because I was a girl. Ouch! So I set off on a long detour, taking me through two marriages, five children, four university degrees, and a career as a feminist economist before I found my true path again. Of course, we can't ever really be off our paths, and everything I learned during those years is important to me today, but the content of my work has changed. As an academic economist, I taught from a spiritual perspective, inspiring students to feel their place in the whole world system, not just their comfortable personal lives. Today I teach a different view of what the whole system looks like. Instead of limiting our human experience to the physical world, I include the non-physical worlds and how we are all united through them.

Finding my true path coincided with leaving a long and difficult marriage. I set out alone with four children under the age of ten. Fortunately I shared parenting with my children's father and I was able to work part-time as a professor. This meant I could devote much of my time to personal healing and development, and to my spiritual growth. I knew my inner calling wasn't to be an economics professor and I knew I could only find my way through deeply transformative work. At first I read widely, joined groups, meditated daily, attended workshops and courses, and explored deeply with different types of healers. Over the early years, I healed the glaring wounds of my personality, developed energetic awareness and learned to obey my spiritual guidance. My true work was slowly revealed to me as spiritual energy healing and the mystical path to God.

As I began learning energy healing, my intuition came on-stream in a big way. As a child I had been highly intuitive and energetically aware. Revisiting these gifts as an adult through meditations, healing work and everyday life, the non-physical worlds opened to me. I saw images, visions, and scenes from peoples' lives, both present and past. I received input from all kinds of spirit guides and Masters. I felt strange sensations throughout my body and my energy field. I saw symbols, heard sounds and had lots of ideas. But what it all was and how I could interpret it accurately where unknown to me. I couldn't reliably tell what was mine and what was other peoples'. I didn't know what to trust and what was only the contribution of my mind. I wanted to use my intuitive skills as a healer and to read the world around me, but my academically trained mind needed to be accurate. I needed the experiences to be both guided and intuitive as well as being consistent, replicable and reliable. I couldn't just pretend I knew what it was all about. I cried out for a spiritual teacher who could guide me in accessing the non-physical dimensions in a systematic way, and help me learn to harness my gift.

At that time, my relationship with nature was the backbone of my spirituality, and so I was led to studying with Tom Brown Jr.[1] Tom had grown up with Stalking Wolf, an Apache spiritual master who taught him the survival, energetic awareness, and spiritual ways of the early people of the Americas. With Tom I learned, among many other things, to become one with the-spirit-that-moves-through-all-things, to track energies in the physical and non-physical dimensions, and to communicate in the spiritual dimensions. I also deepened the value I assigned to living in a fully aware state at all times and in all places.

As my work turned more specifically to esoteric energy healing, I was led to the School of Energy Mastery[2] and Dr. Robert T. Jaffe. Dr. Jaffe had developed a new way of working with the consciousness of energy. He had lived as a mystic as well as being a medical doctor and a homeopath. His Advanced Energy Healing made use of the dimensions of the human energy field. It resonated with the works of Alice Bailey and Djwhal Khul, as well as the energetic understandings of Rosalyn Bruyere and Barbara Brennan. When I first studied with him, he was beginning to walk a Sufi path and his energy healing was deepening into spiritual healing. Through him I learned about the human energy fields, how different aspects of consciousness are found in each field, how conditions of the physical body originate in the non-physical worlds, and how to meet God consciousness directly. Eventually I completed a four-year program to become a certified Advanced Energy Healer.

Putting together all I had learned over many years of study and practice, I gave up the last bits of my regular job as a professor of economics and committed my life totally to the incredible adventure of energy healing and spiritual teaching. My childhood dream had become reality.

I now live a wonderful life, rich with relationships, love and spiritual experience. My children have grown into self-realized, happy people, full of a love for life and faith in their own higher energies that is inspiring. I have been blessed with a profound spiritual partnership and a daily life of gratitude, insight and enlightenment. Through ongoing exploration and integration of spiritual and energetic experience, my life has become more than I could ever have expected. Meanwhile, my understanding of the energy fields and how to live with them and through them continues to expand.

The most obvious way my comprehension grows is in my daily work as a healer. I connect energetically and spiritually with clients, then guide them in knowing their own guidance and embodying their own unique stream of divine consciousness, in healing their wounds and enlightening their energy fields. Each client and each healing is different, yet patterns emerge. Over the years I've facilitated close to ten thousand healings. From applying and adapting information in these healings I have learned a vast amount about the human energy and spiritual fields, and how people can use them.

My work as a spiritual teacher and a teacher of energy healing is another rich field for the further development of ideas. My twenty years as an economics professor has come in handy when figuring out how to teach complicated esoteric material in understandable steps. Over the years I have devised simple exercises to help people access their own spiritual dimensions, learn healing techniques, surrender to a higher order of self and make use of all this energetic information in daily life and relationships. My workshops are collaborative as I believe in cross-fertilization of ideas. I pass along my accumulated knowledge and wisdom to receptive students and together we explore possibilities and map out new information. I have wonderful students from all walks of life, and I can tell from how well they use the information in their own lives that something must be working right.

Another important conduit of information is in the inner planes. I have received countless teachings during meditations and night-time dreams. In meditations, I have been shown new healing techniques, received teachings related to questions I've had, or been 'downloaded' with absolutely new and previously unknown information. I have also experienced energetic initiations into new states of awareness. I also receive direct transmissions of information while I'm asleep. These dream-state teachings are nothing like regular dreams and take many different forms. Sometimes the teaching is obvious and can be integrated into my work immediately. Other times it takes weeks of repeating patterns before the information becomes accessible in the waking state. Many of my most innovative understandings have grown from these direct teachings in the inner planes.

I also learn about the human energy fields through my own healings. I continue to access gifted healers for many types of work and incorporate my knowledge and inner skills into my personal healing experiences. In exploring how I function as an individual, deep truths about humanity are revealed. For years I have journaled my healings, dreams and meditations, keeping track of the teachings to be able to pass the information along to others.

It seems that each person has their own unique set of skills and talents, their own perfect place in the universe. No two people are ever alike. My own special talent seems to be to recognize unseen aspects of life and to quantify and describe them so others can see them too.[3] As a feminist economist, I created new ways of observing hidden parts of the economy including measuring the value of unpaid work, the costs of violence against women, and the economic consequences of child abuse. Now as an energy worker, I have discovered new ways of exploring and describing the human energy fields and spiritual dimensions. It truly seems that passing this information along through writing this book and others to follow is what I was born to do. I hope you enjoy reading it as much as I have enjoyed writing it.

Introduction:
The Nonphysical World

Modern science has somehow measured the total amount of energy that exists in the universe. Surprisingly, the energy captured in the atoms amounts to less than five percent. Those atoms are the material of our human bodies and the physical world we pay so much attention to.[4] But if the physical world only makes up five percent, what else is there? What are the nonphysical dimensions we inhabit?

Consider all the nonphysical aspects of day-to-day life we take for granted. Emotions are not physical, although we may have a body sensation that goes with them. Thoughts aren't physical either. I can think of a pink elephant but there's no corresponding animal standing in my room. Nightly dreams are clearly not physical, although they may have a physical sensation. Intuition is something most people are aware of to some extent; and some people occasionally sense the presence of spiritual beings in their lives, like angels, or a loved one who has died. None of these experiences are purely physical, yet they are regular parts of life. So, where do these nonphysical human experiences come from?

Ancient shamanic knowledge suggests that normal humans only experience about ten percent of reality.[5] Modern science has examined human DNA and mapped less than five percent of its sequencing.[6] This mapped portion represents the total of everything that's known about our bodies and normal experience. The remaining ninety-five percent remains unmapped because no one knows what it relates to.

Proving just what silly humans we really are, the unknown remainder has been referred to as 'junk DNA'.[7] So my questioning begins with "What's going on in the other ninety percent of reality?"

The questions I explore in this book are about the nonphysical dimensions of human experience. What are the nonphysical human energy fields? What is available in our human design other than the aspects we're familiar with? Where do thoughts come from, and where does one find the soul and spirit? And most importantly, how does life change when we live with energetic awareness of all we are?

What I have found is that the nonphysical dimensions of the human experience exist as energy fields that surround and interpenetrate the physical body. Different fields provide information about this lifetime, past lifetimes and various aspects of spirit. They're like nebulous clouds of energy, something like the Earth's magnetic field. The fields are nested one inside the next, with the smallest fields being the densest and most immediate to our experience. It's possible and actually quite easy to become aware of these fields of energy and to begin to work in a conscious, deliberate way with the aspects of self that are housed in each.

This book is designed to teach about the human nonphysical dimensions, to offer various ways of accessing them, and to examine the nature of human experience that's possible if we make the conscious choice to live in full energetic awareness of our whole self. I want to point out that I am writing about something new in our human understanding. To attempt to describe the human energy fields is a somewhat brave undertaking since I know this mapping is certainly not completely accurate. Like the maps of all early explorers, there are certain to be misunderstandings, incorrect proportions and blatant mistakes. Yet early maps can still help people navigate new territories and it is in this context that I would like to share with you what I have discovered.

Unlike those ancient shamans, our modern culture has forgotten much of what it may once have known about the nonphysical dimensions. Instead, we've glorified the workings of the body and the mind, separating them from the rest of life. Through this separation from the world of spirit and energy, we've made mistakes. We look for physical explanations for everything. When children talk with their guides or see energy fields, adults call them imaginary friends or discredit the experience by saying "it's just your imagination". Some people who experience nonphysical reality are considered to be crazy and end up being drugged. When we wonder about the presence on our planet of 'alien' beings we look for actual spacecraft. When people talk about 'body language' they recognize that something subtle is happening, but they interpret it as movements of flesh and bone. When we interpret our world as though everything has a physical explanation we can get into trouble since, without spiritual knowledge, our beliefs are almost certainly wrong.

At the beginning of this new age of human history, we no longer need to be separated from God or Spirit or Life Force, call it what you like. Quantum physics has changed our understanding of what the physical dimension is and spiritual knowledge shows us how to make use of the quantum options. There's enough known about the energetic nonphysical dimensions of reality to enable every human to live in open communication with his or her spiritual nature all the time. But this vision requires us to stop validating our habitual fears and dark beliefs. We have to stop believing the illusion that comes from the separated mind and its physically inspired concepts. The separated mind can no longer be glorified as the provider of 'truth'. The mind is a tool, that's all. It was never meant to replace Spirit. What if truth is 'known' through the subtle bodies, through our energetic connection with our divine spirit? Then, to know spiritual truth, we need to open ourselves to the vast resources of our nonphysical dimensions. Learning to live with energetic awareness will lead us to uncovering a deeper truth for ourselves. Through embodying the spiritual dimensions we can truly live in 'heaven on earth' and create a divine world order with each other.

This book provides a blueprint to follow. It lays out simple information about the nonphysical dimensions of the human energy fields. It offers exercises and meditations to guide you in beginning to experience your own subtle fields. Having worked with this information for a long time, I have discovered that the mind likes this blueprint. It makes sense. It comes to us now for our collective enlightenment. To stop wasting energy from living in a separated state, and to stop our collective suffering, we need to understand our human design.

One wonderful thing about learning the divine blueprint is its applicability. No matter what field of human activity you take it into, it helps. For spiritual seeking, knowing the divine blueprint of the energy fields increases our ability to access mystical experience and know God. For personal growth, knowing the blueprint helps expose the underlying reasons for our issues and problems, and gives us tools to use in healing. For improving personal relationships and creating a better world collectively, knowing the blueprint allows us to understand what makes people behave the way they do with each other. It lets us experience our sameness as humans. We understand ourselves so much better when we look beyond the physical to the subtle dimensions. I invite you to join me in developing your own energetic awareness through exploring your own nonphysical dimensions.

Chapter One

Becoming Conscious of Consciousness

In our everyday world, human experience is limited mainly to thoughts, feelings and actions. These are the functions of the personality of this lifetime. Most people never knowingly engage with the subtle fields of their souls and spirits. They don't know the fields exist or how to access them. Normal choices end up being limited to only a few of the functions humans are designed to experience. My purpose here is to introduce you to the rest of your self, to your unknown but always present dimensions, so your choices can expand to include everything that's possible in our human design.

To begin exploring the existence of the subtle fields, let's explore what we're really made of. Sit quietly for a moment and feel into yourself. Take a deep breath and relax. Now feel into yourself. What are you? You have a body, but you can't be only your body since you can tell your body what to do. Your body might change, as bodies do, through age or by accident, but you would still be you. Even if you could have an operation and get a brand-new body, like an artificial limb, you would still be you. Your looks would change, and the options available to you in the outside world might change, but you would still be you.

No matter what happens to your body, as long as you are still alive, you are still you.

If you aren't just your body, then maybe you're a combination of your body and your feelings. Take a moment now and feel into your emotions. How are you feeling emotionally at this moment in time? Content, anxious, angry, happy ...? You can have any emotional feeling, but that won't define what you are either. Emotions are the workings of the emotional body. You can feel happy or sad, cheerful or humiliated and it's still you having the experience. Emotions are vital to the experience of being human, but they aren't the experience itself.

If you aren't only your body and your feelings, maybe you are also your mind. Take a moment and sense your mind. What is it busy paying attention to right now? ... this book ... a fly at the window ... what to eat for supper ... You can have any thoughts, but it's still you having them. Thoughts don't define what you are either; they're only the workings of your mental apparatus. You can think anything, in concrete terms or abstractly, about facts, experiences or desires, and you will still be you. You can change what you think about things, and you may experience yourself and your world differently as a result, but you will still be you.

While your body, feelings and thoughts are all important parts of you, there is still a fundamental, underlying self that is having all the experiences. Let's call this fundamental aspect your consciousness, awareness or spirit. This consciousness or awareness of self underlies all thought, feelings or action. No matter what else is going on, this underlying consciousness is present. So let's begin by saying we are each an unending stream of spirit consciousness, housed in a body, with a bunch of tools to use to explore life. Take a moment and bring your awareness to this consciousness that defines the underlying you.

Consciousness as Raw Material

Consciousness is a vast and mysterious topic. Although consciousness has been the domain of mystics since humanity began, it has only recently become a topic for western scientific investigation. Scientists used to believe that if we could understand time, space and matter perfectly, then we could see how consciousness was created. But in the words of quantum physicist Peter Russell, there is a new meta-paradigm emerging in science that recognizes that consciousness is primary.[8] Consciousness has created time, space and matter and not the other way around. Consciousness is in everything and everything is in consciousness. This is the Oneness of mystical experience. It is the raw material not only of individuals, but of all organisms and all groups. I like to think of consciousness as the body of God.

This consciousness is each person's raw material. This awareness is at the core of our nature and is basically the same for each of us. In spirit, we all have the same quality of beingness. In God, there is only One of us. But from the moment of conception we make different choices of how to use this raw material. It is the history of our choices that differentiates us from each other. We each embody a unique version of the collective potential.

Because our stream of consciousness exists in every moment, it must be spent. What we do with it ends up defining our specific reality. We can think thoughts, feel feelings and perform actions. We can sleep, meditate or play. We can shift our awareness into an expanded dimension and perceive our lives from a more spiritually inspired perspective. The choices are infinite. But whatever we choose in the timestream of moments, our choice gets recorded in our subtle bodies and creates our own unique reality. We become living reflections of our consciousness stream and the history of choices we have made, both individually and collectively.

Let's look at how this happens. At this moment you're choosing the activity of looking at this book but your awareness may or may not be connecting with the words. You might be handling the book, wondering whether it's worth buying. Or you might really be paying attention to how your foot hurts, or how excited you feel about something. Or you may be zoned out, disconnected from physical stimulus, feeling numb with exhaustion. Consciousness includes all options. Which option you choose is up to you. If you are thinking, which most humans spend most of their time doing, then thinking is the activity you're choosing for your consciousness right now. Thinking isn't the only option though. You could be daydreaming, meditating or falling asleep while your eyes track these words and you might not be thinking at all. Yet you are still experiencing yourself through your stream of consciousness while handling this book.

Now let's suppose you are thinking, and that you're also choosing to pay attention to the words written here. As you pay attention, you have your own unique mental experience. What your mind does with the words depends on all the previous choices you've made and the resulting thoughts available to you in this moment. What your mind does with the ideas will be different from what every other person who reads this book does with them. You will absorb exactly what you choose from the words. Each person has their own unique mental body just as we each have a unique physical body. The thoughts you have become part of your reality, different from everyone else's, and what you do with them is entirely your own choice. You create your own inner reality through the moment-by-moment choice of your thoughts.

Making Things Matter

Whatever you choose to pay attention to, in that moment you make the choice matter by bringing the results of it into your world. You materialize it. You may be materializing it physically, or you may be materializing it as structures in your mental body. Whatever your choice of the moment, it becomes part of your reality.

If I'm hungry and I choose to make a sandwich, I make it matter. I 'matter' it by materializing the sandwich in the physical world. Likewise, if I'm hurting emotionally and I choose to think my friend is at fault, my belief matters to me and I materialize my belief in my world. Since we are all one in spirit, making the belief matter in my reality actually brings it into my friend's reality too. Whether or not I act outwardly on the basis of my belief, I create it for both of us. My friend might be unaware of it, but it is still subtly present in his or her field. If I decide to act physically on the basis of my belief, I make it matter in the physical world too. Now my friend is more likely to notice it, and so I have materialized it in my friend's physical and mental reality as well.

So we are made. What we spend our consciousness doing reflects itself back to us from our personal and collective reality. This is the nature of our design. The choices exist whether we pay attention to them or not. Unfortunately, we often live as though we were victims of our own thought processes, feeling helpless to change our internal behavior. Yet this is not so. Pretending to ourselves that we don't have choice over what we do with our consciousness is a tragedy. Instead, it is possible to live in an on-going state of awareness in which we notice options and choose on purpose how to spend our consciousness.

The Power of Choice

Even when we think we have no choice, we still have infinite choices, because on the inside we are never helpless. In the physical dimension, there might be conditions we can't change; for example, prisoners can't leave jail and children can't live alone. But even when we can't change the physical dimension, we still have vast choices in the other dimensions. It is the internal choice of what to pay attention to that determines the nature of our lives. It is said that Jews in the concentration camps often used this inner choice as their point of strength. Although their bodies could be deprived of all physical needs, it was up to the individual how they reacted. They could still die with their dignity intact.[9] Or think of the Gary Larson cartoon in which a fellow is pushing a wheelbarrow full of ashes in Hell while whistling happily. One of the devils says "We're just not reaching that guy."[10] We always have inner choices. We can choose to change what's possible, or to feel angry and unhappy. We can choose to stay loving, or to think dark thoughts. I see this as the great teaching of Jesus on the cross: we can have the worst possible thing happen to us, to be tortured to death, yet we can still stay connected with love and forgiveness rather than go to dark thoughts of hatred and revenge. The choice is ours.

When people live from awareness, they are in their own power. They have access to the mechanisms of conscious life. They are not uncontrollably swept along by outer currents, but make deliberate choices to experience life in a way that suits them. They can follow their own inner truth with stability and grace. They can know true happiness and satisfaction. If they are bothered by negative thoughts and feelings, they can face their inner reality and enable new solutions to arise. In the divine plan for humanity we are all vital, fully aware Beings, living with deliberate choice over what to do with our unique streams of consciousness, and co-creating collective reality as fully conscious humans.

We're beginning here to develop a sense of what we humans really are and how we choose to live. We are unique versions of Spirit consciousness, going about the business of creating our daily lives. We think thoughts, have feelings and move our bodies about. We have soul-level experiences, although we may not recognize them as such. We have access to everything that's available in all the spiritual dimensions, although most of us don't choose to explore the spiritual realms very much. We each represent the collection of all our previous choices, from this lifetime and others. In any moment we have immeasurable choice available to us; and yet we live as though this were not true. Most of us only pay attention to the physical dimension and the personality level. We think if something isn't physical, then it isn't real. We get caught in the structure of our mental bodies, believing our beliefs, and following habits of thought laid down long ago. We overrate our minds, confusing them with our spirit consciousness itself. In this way we rob ourselves of the creative joy of being human. We also rob ourselves of ninety percent of what's possible.

Once we're aware of our stream of consciousness, we can begin to choose how to use it. We can choose to explore our vast selves and materialize experiences from our soul and spirit dimensions. We can live in the present moment instead of only re-visiting past thoughts that are stored in our mental bodies. In order to make choices though, we need to know what's possible. What is there to choose from? The options in our human design are vast. We're very complicated and sophisticated beings. We can choose to pay attention to our emotions, our thoughts, our soul level input or our spiritual input. We can choose which dimension to be aware of, and we can recognize incoming stimulus from any of the fields. And we can connect with friends in the physical and nonphysical dimensions. Our options are infinite. In the following chapters we explore the energetic dimensions in more detail in order to expand what's possible.

Practical Exercises

Spiritual growth isn't something we can think our way to. It needs to happen as a felt experience. To feel spirit, we have to engage with more of the energetic dimensions of our complex fields than only our mental bodies. We have to let the energetic experiences actually happen, and not just think about them or visualize them. For this reason I offer you some exercises and meditations to explore so the teachings in this book will take on more meaning for you than just the conceptual aspects.

- *Moving your Point of Awareness*

The basic skill involved in these exercises is the ability to move your point of awareness around through your body and your energy field. Notice that you have a location, or a center point of your awareness, like a point of active consciousness. To start, relax and feel your body wherever you are right now. Take your time. Slow down your rate of internal activity from the fast, electrical activity of thinking to the slower, gentler speed of awareness. What position are you in? What areas feel comfortable or uncomfortable? Pay full attention and really notice what it feels like. Now bring your awareness to your clothing, maybe layers of clothing. The action of moving your awareness feels like a gathering together of attention or of noticing into a specific location. Now bring your awareness to your breath moving in and out of your chest. Notice the in-breath and the out-breath. Now notice the turning point where the in-breath turns into the out-breath and the out-breath turns into the in-breath. Now see if you can elongate that turning, really sinking into it and letting it lengthen. Just witness the breath without actively thinking about it.

Now move your point of awareness to your forehead. How does your forehead feel from inside? Now move your point of awareness down into your throat. How does your throat feel from the inside? Now move your point of active consciousness down into your hand that's holding this book. What does your hand feel like from inside? Now bring your awareness into your heart and open yourself to any feeling that arises.

Take a few minutes and play with moving your point of awareness around through your body. An important aspect of learning to have energy awareness is to realize you have an energetic geography and it's possible to move your consciousness around to different locations. Make sure you aren't just imagining it from your head but actually moving the location of your awareness. You can tell by what it feels like. If you're in your head, you won't feel anything at all. Your experience will be limited to thoughts or concepts or pictures. As you actually move your point of awareness around, you will feel different energetic sensations such as pressure or motion, heat or tingling. You may feel expansive or contracted places, colors or darkness. You may observe energetic patterns like abstract art, or odd visions may pop up at you. You may also feel emotions or experience memories. Energy is very varied and never the same from one location to the next. Flow with it and just notice. There's nothing for you to do with the energies just yet except to receive impressions of sensation. Describing it is like describing abstract art. Words, after all, were made up to describe the ten percent of reality we're already familiar with, so they can only point towards the sensation of energy and never really capture it.

- *Witnessing your Energetic Reactions*

Now feel your whole body as you rest with this book. Get an overall sensation of your energy field or aura, whatever that means to you. Explore it quietly, noticing how it feels and give it a description of some kind ... Any description will do. This is just between you and you. Now, observe how your energy field reacts if you trigger yourself by thinking of something you really dislike. It can be a food or smell or person or event. Notice that it isn't physical sensations of your body you're observing because the object doesn't exist in the physical dimension right now. But you may notice areas that energetically contract, twist, get flat or cold or darken. Observe how your energy field is reacting to the thought of the thing you dislike. Don't pay attention to your thoughts or emotions. Just notice how your energy field changes shape and texture. After you've investigated for long enough to have a feeling for these changes, relax entirely and clear your mind of all the negative stimulus. Come back to observing your body resting wherever you are and again observe the changes in your energy field ... Now observe how your field responds to the release of tension. Does it revert to its original state easily or does it hang on to the more negative reaction?

Now start again from the neutral state of just observing your whole field, breath deeply and this time trigger the opposite experience by thinking of something you really like or love, be it a person, pet, place, food or whatever. Observe again how your field changes. It will probably expand, grow bigger, get lighter or feel tingly or warm. Again you can play with this a bit by considering other people or places that you really love. Keep exploring the subtle sensations of how your energy field shifts and flows in accordance with your thoughts. Notice meanwhile that your body hasn't changed at all. Your heart rate, temperature and physical position won't have altered much at all.

Noticing how your energy field is responding to the experiences of your life is an important step toward living a more aware existence. It takes a little time and attention to notice these subtle feelings, but once you catch on to it, you'll discover your energy field is giving you important feedback all the time about the choices you're making concerning how to spend your consciousness.

- 'Coming In' from the Mental Body

The next step in creating choice is to learn how to access the non-physical dimensions of your energy fields on purpose. To do this, you need to disengage your active mind. Our mental apparatus gets in the way of feeling the subtle bodies. The mental body is most easily felt out around the head, usually in front of the forehead. To feel the activity of your mental body, notice where your point of awareness has reverted to as you begin to read this book again. It almost certainly has rebounded to your head or forehead. This makes sense since we use our minds to take in written information. Reading this book pulls your point of awareness into the mental body of your third eye chakra. To release your consciousness from the mental body, do the following exercise. I suggest you read the instructions all the way through, doing the process bit by bit. Then close your eyes and do it again. It may take a few attempts to still the mind.

First, bring all your awareness up to your forehead. Now imagine there's a gentle vacuum running all across your whole brow, and it's gently sucking in. Let your point of awareness be drawn in, in, in. Come in behind your forehead, behind your eyeballs, to deep within. You're actually moving your awareness into the central column of energy that runs from the north pole to the south pole of your energy field. If you feel a lot of motion or density, just keep pulling in further until you get behind those feelings. Once your point of awareness has come inside, just rest there a while until you feel like coming back out to the book. Now close your eyes and do it again. Forehead, vacuum, deep within.

* * * * * * * * *

If you succeeded in having this experience you probably feel more relaxed now, or peaceful. What was it like to disengage from the mental body? Did you feel relaxed and disconnected from your concerns? Did your mind get in the way, talking to you about why you shouldn't or couldn't do this exercise? Or did your inner critic jump in to say you might as well not even bother trying because you'll do it wrong no matter what, or you don't have time to waste on this nonsense? Did your brow knit together in an attempt to keep you locked out in the mental body where it feels familiar? Or did you slip easily through, seeming to pop into a different dimension of the self where nothing matters quite the same way it seems to in normal life? If you are a regular meditator, you probably experienced what it feels like to enter into the meditative state. If your meditations are happening in the front of your head, consider trying it this way for a while. You'll probably have more energetic connection with your inner experiences.

Remember, spiritual growth isn't something we can think our way to. It has to happen as an experience. Relax and breathe deeply. Let's do the exercise again, and this time, allow yourself to go further in than before. Unhook from your mind, and observe yourself as a stream of consciousness making choices in the moment. If you meet with interference or resistance from negative thoughts, just notice what's happening without judging it. You can always ask your spiritual self to help too. Remember, after closing your eyes, bring your awareness to your forehead; imagine a gentle vacuum, and let yourself be drawn inside, deep in, behind the forehead and eyes. If you get into a tight spot or anything uncomfortable, just keep going until you get behind that, but without going out the back of your head. Stay deep within, experiencing the subtle energies of your central core. Then just sit and notice the choices you make as to how to spend your stream of consciousness moment by moment. Notice that having a thought will pull you back out the front. Just repeat the exercise, coming deep in behind the eyes and witness your consciousness again.

* * * * * * * * *

I love the feeling within these deep places. It is peaceful and quiet. Different things matter here, like love, and being receptive. Notice that you still have thoughts, but they don't lead your experience, they follow it. This is the first step in any meditation. Come in to yourself. Come in, and disengage from the mental body. Come home to your spiritual energies deep in the core of your body. We can learn to live from this inner channel. All the abilities of the personality still exist, but our experience is not limited to them. You can explore with this skill. Imagine the vacuum, suck your awareness deep within behind the forehead and eyeballs, and slowly open your eyes again. See how it feels to be there in your 'real life' with more than your mental body engaged. As you practice and find it easier to get inside, go and do simple tasks from this state. Meditation is not meant to be an end in itself, but a way of living all the time. It becomes possible to live fully from this inner place. You need never be locked out in the mental body again.

Chapter Two

Overview of the Human Energy Fields

To be able to choose from all the possible experiences we have as conscious humans, we need to know what's available. This chapter provides a quick overview of the spiritual dimensions and a more in-depth look at the role of the chakras in consciousness. Later chapters go into more detail for each of the dimensions and include exercises on how to access them. The final chapters explore how life changes as we integrate the nonphysical dimensions into our lives.

Perceiving the Energy Fields

As humans, we are blessed with the ability to experience both the subtle and the dense. This combination is part of our special design. We use our physical body to experience the physical world, our emotional body to experience the world of emotions and our mental body to create thoughts. We use our soul fields to engage with other souls and our spiritual bodies to experience the worlds of spirit. Becoming aware of our own subtle bodies enables us to access the experiences in all the dimensions we inhabit.

We know what our physical body is like since we perceive it with our physical senses. To know what our energy fields are like, we need to perceive them with our energetic senses. The skills of our energetic senses, such as clairvoyance and clairsentience, can be developed in anyone since the ability is inherent in our design. While many people aim to perceive energy through the visual function of their third eye chakra, there are easier and more universal skills you can develop to perceive your whole energy field. However, it takes time to learn. The exercises in this book will help you to lay down the basic skills for energetic perception. In the meantime, I will share with you both what I have perceived and descriptions of what many other people have perceived about the energy fields. Each person senses energy slightly differently and all ways of perceiving are valid. When a number of people compare what they perceive, they are usually perceiving the same thing, but in slightly different ways.

What do the human energy fields look like? In their simplest forms, they look like irregularly shaped spheres with an open column running down the middle. They're toroidal in shape, like a tall donut. They resemble the Earth's magnetic field, with a north and south pole and an open core running through the center. Each person's field is made up of a number of these dimensions increasing in size from small to very vast. Although they are donut shaped, for convenience I'll refer to them as spheres or fields. The smaller spheres are nested within the larger ones. Each sphere houses a different dimension with a different structure and appearance, a different quality of consciousness and a different purpose. They look different, feel different, sound different and provide different experiences. Each dimension houses a different template of consciousness. As you work with these expanded dimensions, you will gain familiarity with each of them and eventually recognize the signature template of each of the fields.

Figure 1 is an artist's schematic cutaway of the different dimensions, not drawn to scale.* The proper scale would show the fields getting much larger the farther from the physical body they are. Imagine each

---

* To see more illustrations, and for more information on the energy fields and energy awareness, please visit www.solaria.ws/twy.

field as an irregular sphere and allow them all to co-exist in the same geographic location in time and space. Imagine it like one of those old books of the Visible Man in which each layer is on a transparency and you can lay them down one on top of the other. Together, they make up the whole. Any one layer can also be viewed and explored on its own. The fields are nested one inside the next, from the smallest and densest to the largest and most expanded. This means they all exist within each atom. The expanded dimensions co-exist within the denser ones, so they all exist in the same location. Moving from one to another in the body involves shifting consciousness deeper into a particular spot. It feels like deepening awareness, or making phase transitions from one state of being to another.

Figure 1 - Layers of the Human Energy Fields

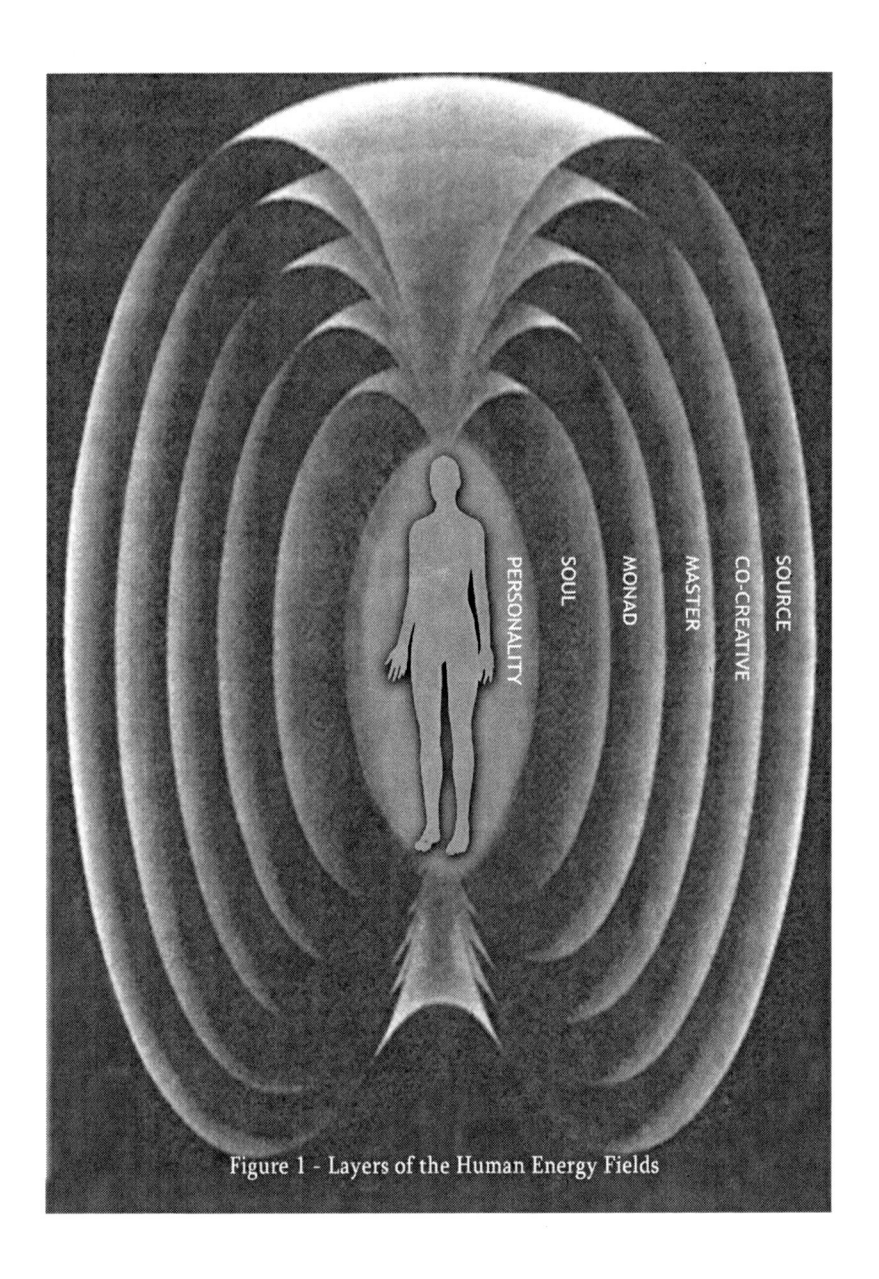

Each dimension is energetically different from all the others. It seems the vast spiritual dimensions vibrate at the highest frequencies, while the physical dimension vibrates at the lowest frequency. As the dimensions become larger, more expanded and less densely structured, the quality of their conscious experience changes, becoming more expanded, more subtle, more loving and much more powerful. Density goes with intensity while subtlety goes with true power. The most expanded and powerful field is the source energy we call God. It is the overarching, largest field, and is infinitely powerful. Everything else is nested within it. So God is in everything, and everything is in God.

The smallest of the energy spheres is the physical body. We may think of it as solid, but it is still made of energy, in tightly packed, swirling atoms. The physical dimension is the densest of the energy fields, and from our human perspective, the most intense. If you cut your arm, it hurts in a very intense way. It would be hard to meditate in the subtler fields if your arm was hurting because the dense dimensions demand more attention in the human experience. The ability to overcome physical pain through meditative processes takes time to develop.

The Layers of Dimensions

As stated above, the dimensions all exist in the same location, and it's possible to move your point of awareness through each one to the next. The densest layers are directly related to the physical body and this lifetime of experience. These are known as the personality level and include the physical body, the emotional body and the mental body. This field makes up the everyday experiences we are used to. Combined together the personality measures about two to three feet across, sticking out about five inches beyond the physical body. This field feels like our personal 'space' and we instinctively back away if a stranger gets too close to it, while we invite our intimate friends and family into it through hugging or cuddling. When an individual dies, these layers no longer exist as they're fundamentally connected to the experiences of this physical life. In chapter 3, I go into more detail about the mental and emotional bodies.

The next biggest dimension is the human soul level. The structure of the soul field is more finely textured and feels further away than the personality levels. It measures about four or five feet across, or approximately arms-length out from the body. The soul dimension includes all past life experiences of humanity. The soul has an individual component as well as a collective one. When a person is in a healing and they suddenly recall a past-life story from a different time and place in history, their consciousness has shifted into their soul level. Core fears and beliefs that make little sense given an individual's life story usually stem from patterns in the soul. It may be true that individual souls reincarnate from one lifetime to another, or it may be that spirit chooses aspects of humanity at the beginning of a lifetime like ladling soup from a pot. It may be that all of humanity is one great Being, experiencing itself through myriad lifetimes of experience, or it could be that each individual life is a unique and completely separate experience. It doesn't really matter which paradigm you choose to relate to the soul field. The only verifiable information is that the field does exist and it does house stories from the history of humanity. You can conceive of it however you are most comfortable. I will usually refer to soul-level experiences as past-life experiences, but recognize that this could mean lifetimes of the individual or of all humanity.

The soul also houses an etheric template for the physical body. This template functions as a blueprint to be used for growing our bodies or repairing damaged tissue. The template can be accessed intentionally for healing. When a person has an injury, the template can be engaged to help the cells remember their normal state. Physical healing then occurs much faster and more cleanly. There can also be conditions in the etheric template itself from previous life experiences which can get re-initiated in this lifetime. They might turn up as birth defects, genetic diseases that come on later in life, or as unexplained weaknesses. The etheric template itself can be healed by accessing the past life experience in which the original condition was formed and engaging the original undamaged template. In chapter 5, I go in detail into the nature of the soul level and the etheric template.

Beyond the human soul level come fields of pure spirit energy. In the esoteric traditions the first spiritual dimension is called the Monad, which means 'One'. The size of the monadic field varies between individuals but is roughly ten or twelve feet across. The monad can be thought of as the unconditionally loving Higher Self. It steps down huge spiritual energies toward life taking a soul or physical form. The higher energies of the Monad are always loving, peaceful and supportive. When a person connects with their monadic energies, they experience a profoundly compassionate and calm attitude toward life. It has been described as 'the peace that passes all understanding'. The monad also has a very expanded collective feeling. For many people, experiencing the monad is the first taste of feeling the Oneness of God. The monad feels wise and reliably unconditional in its love of the soul and personality. It is the part of the self that witnesses the play of physical existence from outside the illusion of the human experience.

Beyond the Monad come vast spiritual dimensions, each more expanded and powerful than the ones nested within. These dimensions are rarely accessed in normal human life. Sometimes they become available to a person during a meditation or healing. While it is possible, it's rare for someone to incorporate the expanded fields into their regular life, since that's not what normal human activity is all about. However, at this time of enlightenment and ascension of humanity, many more people are beginning to work from these dimensions. It's time to know what they are, how to access them, and to begin integrating them consciously and deliberately into the fabric of human life.

The first dimension beyond the monadic I call the Master level. It is the command center for the work of Spirit on the planet. When the Higher Self expands to the Master level, the spiritual work takes over all aspects of the person's life. The individual has an open flow of communication with Spirit, and is able to bring God consciousness through for all humanity. Every human could recognize and resonate with the flow of teachings, regardless of their personal beliefs. The energies of the Ascended Masters are found in this dimension. Master level energies can also cascade through a musician or artist who is fully open to channel the energy of Spirit through their work.

The next dimension in our energy fields I call the co-creative level. I offer in this book the small amount I've come to understand about this dimension. As I've said before, this information may or may not be 'correct', but it still seems useful as a starting point. I expect that over time, more and more knowledge of these higher spiritual dimensions will be revealed to us here in the human world and we can share what we know. The co-creative dimension seems to be where unified consciousness begins separating toward all life everywhere. All the big spiritual dimensions begin here. The originating streams of energy are vast beyond comprehension, moving towards creating life in its myriad forms. All the different universes originate from this dimension. These universes can be made of light or sound, and can make use of consciousness in ways that are totally different from the way humanity uses consciousness.

Beyond all these dimensions comes our unified consciousness in which we are God as a single being. There is only one self, with countless expressions. The expressions are constantly changing and evolving. The self is conscious, creative love. This is the Absolute, from which all else forms.

The Chakra System

In order to understand the blueprint of the subtle dimensions, and to live fully integrated with all our spiritual aspects, we also need to know something about the chakra system. In their technical aspects, chakras are vortices of flowing energy that move spiritual currents through the subtle bodies. The opening looks a bit like the iris of an eye, able to open wider or close down more tightly. There are seven major chakras within the physical body and more extending above. The higher chakras are the openings in the center of each energy field, and can be very wide open or almost closed entirely. They function as valves, opening the smaller fields to the spiritual energies beyond. Each layer has a corresponding chakra below the feet as well, where the energy from beyond flows up. The major chakras in the physical body are more complex since they also contain a horizontal flow of energy. You can see an artist's schematic impression of the chakra openings in Figure 2.

Chakra openings look something like water swirling down a drain or the air of a tornado. They swirl in constant motion. In a person who is blocked and tight, the openings can be small. The vortex may also be misshapen or lumpy. In a person who is relaxed and at peace in their life, the opening will likely be wider and more circular. Each chakra has an emotional body and a mental body component, as well as soul and monadic level aspects. The more spiritual energy a person has integrated into their field, the wider open the chakras will be.

Chakras Come in Sets of Three

But chakras are not mere technical devices for moving energy. They are also tools of consciousness. There is a pattern repeated throughout all the dimensions in which there are always three layered chakras, like Neapolitan ice-cream. The bottom chakra is an anchor that brings in and anchors all the higher spiritual energies into that dimension. The middle one is an extroverted, relationship chakra that connects with other beings in that dimension, and the upper one is an introverted, personal chakra that provides a sense of self within that dimension. No matter what dimension of life we are engaged with, there is always a personal aspect and a relational aspect. The chakra system helps us to understand that life is all about self and others.

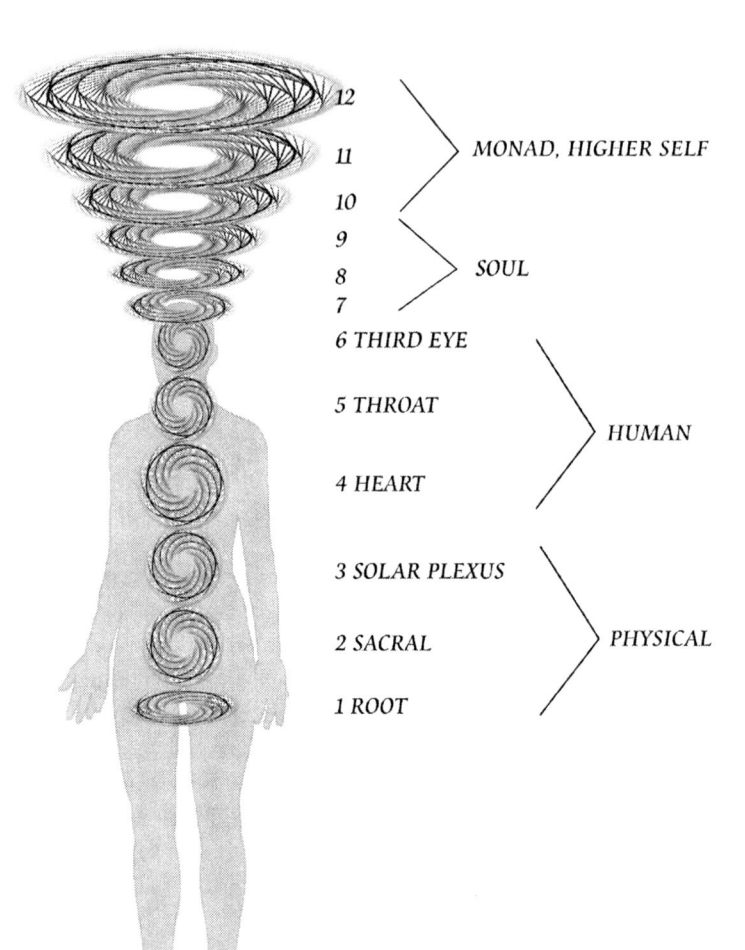

Figure 2 - Schematic Impression of the Chakra System

Each of the seven chakras contains a whole area of the physical body, so every cell of the body is housed in one or another of the chakras. The bottom three are related to living in the physical dimension. The first or root chakra includes the feet and legs, up to the perineum and base of the hips. It is the anchor that holds all the higher spiritual energies in the physical dimension and gives us the physical body. The second or sacral chakra is the abdomen between the hips and the waist and is the relational, extroverted chakra of the physical dimension. The third or solar plexus chakra extends from the waist to the diaphragm and is the personal, or introverted center of the physical self.

The next set of three chakras house the dimension of human experience. The fourth or heart chakra extends through the ribcage and the underside of the arms and hands, up to the collarbones. It is the place where all the higher spirit energies anchor into human experience. The fifth or throat chakra includes the top of the hands, arms and shoulders, the throat and face up to the cheekbones and ears. It is the relational, extroverted chakra of our human experience. The sixth or third eye chakra includes the eyes and the whole head up to the crest of the skull on which a crown would rest and is the introverted, personal chakra of the human experience.

The seventh or crown chakra, at the top of the head, is the anchoring chakra of the soul dimension, with the eighth and ninth being the extroverted and introverted aspects of the human soul. The tenth chakra, about an arms-length above the head, anchors the higher energies into our monadic, higher self. The eleventh and twelfth then are the relational and personal chakras of the higher self, and so on. Let's now take a more detailed look at the nature of consciousness housed in each chakra.

The Seven Body Chakras

Each chakra houses a different aspect of our human nature and is quite distinct from the others. As we live our lives, every experience is felt in every chakra, but different aspects of the experience are felt in the different chakras. For example, suppose you were at a gathering in a strange place, at which you had to speak on a topic you cared deeply about. Your root chakra would relate to the location, your sacral to the people, and your solar plexus to how good a job you felt you were doing. Your heart would relate to the passion of your message, your throat would express your views, and your third eye would work to figure the whole thing out. Your crown would keep you connected to your higher self and your spiritual purpose for being there. If something difficult happened, each chakra would store the experience in the context of its own energies. Let's examine those energies in more detail.

The first, or Root chakra, connects the entire spirit self into the physical dimension of our planet. The root gives us a physical body and the ability to move it about. It demonstrates our comfort at being alive in a body. People who don't like being human, who connect deeply into the suffering on the planet, or who wish to be able to 'go home' spiritually often have very thin root chakras. They haven't really made their peace with being here in a body and being human. People who have had a life-threatening accident or illness often have a distortion in the root since they lived through the threat of losing their physical body. The root literally keeps body and soul together. When a person is dying, their spiritual energy moves up and out of the root first, and the person becomes bed-ridden or they fall down. The root also reflects our relationship with the physical dimension regarding money and abundance since not having enough money can be a survival issue. It also holds the patterns of our relationship with the Earth. A person who is comfortable sitting on the ground and getting dirty is likely to have a more open root chakra than someone who is only comfortable in high-heeled shoes in a high rise building. A healthy root chakra is wide open, allowing all the expanded subtle fields to be anchored through the human body into the physical dimension.

The second chakra, called the Sacral chakra, is the relational or connecting chakra of the physical self. It manages our relationship energies with other people in the physical world. Patterns in the second chakra reflect our habits of relationship. A person who is afraid of other people and protects him or herself through distance or avoidance will probably have a blocked or shielded second. A person who is extroverted and enjoys connecting with other people will likely have an open, flowing second chakra. A person who is co-dependent or needy around other people may send out tendrils from their second chakra that seek to entwine into other people's fields and attach there. Sexual intercourse brings the second chakras together in a physical connection. Some people use sexual energy in most of their second chakra connections, often without being aware they are doing so. This can cause mixed messages if they don't want to be sexually engaged with another person. A healthy sacral chakra is open and flowing, allowing energies from other people to move through and be felt, without attaching to them or distancing from them.

The third chakra, or Solar Plexus, is the individuated or personal chakra of the physical human. It is the seat of our self-identity. In the third chakra we house our self-confidence, self-esteem and self-worth. If these energies are not healthy in a person's life, then his or her solar plexus will likely be tight and uncomfortable. The solar plexus is where we house the will to live our lives in accordance with what's right for us as individuals. It is our internal power center. Some people use their own solar plexus energies to attempt to control the behaviour of other people. Arguments almost always have both participants locked into the solar plexus, each attempting to exert his or her will on the outcome of the fight. The solar plexus represents our own domain in which we are sovereign. A self-respecting human will work to restore what's right for him or herself if someone else is invading their solar plexus territory. Otherwise he or she may collapse into a state of disempowerment that allows the other person's will to dictate. A healthy solar plexus houses a robust sense of self and an awareness of what's right and wrong for the self.

The fourth chakra is the Heart. It is the bottom of the three chakras of the human dimension and as such anchors the higher spiritual energies into the human experience. Since Spirit is love, the Heart is all about love. Through the Heart we feel and know love, compassion and caring. We feel gratitude and generosity. The heart is the center of faith, hope and trust. Every human loves others, and wants to be loved by others. Love is the human constant. Through feeling love, we experience the presence of God. When people turn their backs on a person or group and don't connect lovingly with them, they have closed their heart chakras to the others. This separates them from knowing God in the other people. When the Heart has been betrayed or hurt in some way, an individual often closes or blocks the chakra in an attempt to protect him or herself from more pain. With a blocked chakra, the person can't feel love flowing in or out. This prevents them from loving others fully, and from receiving the love that's there for them in their lives. They will usually feel a sense of separation and isolation. When a person doesn't love himself, he can't know God in himself. A person with an open Heart chakra feels kind and generous, and is easy to be around. He gives and receives love easily. Energies from the Heart chakra extend down the underside of the arms and hands. Loving touch, holding hands and hugs are all gestures of the Heart.

When a person is dying, it is possible to observe how the spiritual energies move out from the root chakra up. If the person is dying of old age or a long-term sickness, you can observe the process happening. The person slows down and eventually becomes bed-ridden. Their legs may get cold and bluish. As the energies move up through the second chakra, the person may lose bladder or bowel control. Closer to death, the energies will move up through the solar plexus and the digestive system may stop functioning. A person can stay alive without much energy in the lower three chakras. However, once the anchoring of spirit moves from the heart, the person can no longer stay in the body. As the energies begin moving out of the Heart chakra, breathing becomes labored and the physical heart beats more slowly. The energies finally move up and out, past the heart chakra, and the person is no longer alive in their body. The Root anchors spirit into the physical dimension of the planet, but the Heart anchors spiritual energies into the human experience. It anchors love into form. Once the energy has moved above the Heart, spirit can no longer be connected into the human experience.

Throughout history there have been certain spiritual sages who have existed without eating food or drinking water.[11] These individuals have moved all the energy out of their lower three chakras without continuing to move out through the heart. They are able to disconnect energetically from the physical dimension while staying rooted as spirit in the dimension of human experience. These people exist by feeding their bodies the energy they need directly from spirit rather than through the mechanisms of atomic and molecular structure. Normally, energy is captured in atoms and molecules, then transferred to the body through food and water. However, energy can be fed to the body through the etheric structure on the soul levels without needing the physical input. To live such an existence probably requires a profound relationship with God and Spirit energy.

Let's continue now to look at the chakras that represent the human experience. The fifth chakra is the Throat. It is the relational chakra of the human experience and is therefore the seat of self-expression in the physical dimension. We express ourselves to the outer world through our voices and through all forms of creative expression. We communicate through the throat. The throat chakra includes the face up to the cheekbones, the ears, the throat, the tops of the shoulders and the back of the arms and hands. That means that what we show on our faces and how we listen are actions of the throat chakra, as well as all movements we make for music, painting, cooking, writing or any other creative activity. People who feel free to express their truth in any way that suits them and who let their creativity flow will likely have open throat chakras. People who are afraid to talk or express themselves, who fear making a mess or 'doing it wrong' will likely have closed throat chakras. A healthy throat chakra is a vibrant, open flow of incoming and outgoing communication.

The sixth chakra is called the Third Eye. It is the seat of individual human awareness and perception. Through it a person thinks, contemplates, envisions and dreams. The third eye chakra houses personal human consciousness and the personal mind. It is the access point into the mental body which stores conscious memory and through which a person analyzes life. A person who enjoys thinking, who has good self-awareness, and who is open-minded will likely have an open third eye. A person who thinks of him or herself as stupid, who feels confused a lot of the time, or is dogmatically closed-minded will almost certainly have a tight third eye. The third eye is also the seat of clairvoyance or the ability to perceive energies. The physical eyes are in the third eye chakra and it is through them that we perceive physical objects. Similarly, it is through the subtle dimensions of the third eye that we perceive the subtle fields.

At the top of the head is the first of the soul level chakras, the Crown chakra. It anchors all the expanded dimensions of the human spirit into the human soul. An open Crown chakra enables the higher realms of spirit energy to be felt in the human experience. If a person's Crown chakra is closed or blocked, he or she will live a life limited to the personality level of experience. There will be no felt awareness of spiritual energies. The person might still have a nice heart, a mental belief in God and flowing chakras, although this is unlikely, but they won't have a felt experience of their spiritual energies. They will more likely feel cut-off from life. Usually when the Crown is closed the person is susceptible to depression and negativity. They often feel isolated and separate and suffer from a lot of fear. This is because the love, comfort and support that Spirit brings into human life is cut off. Left on our own in the human world can be a depressing experience because of the fear, oppression and suffering we encounter. Staying connected with Spirit through having an open, flowing Crown chakra helps us to feel part of a bigger picture. In later chapters, I explore in detail how to connect and stay connected with the subtle fields.

In the following chapters I explore each of the dimensions in more detail and show you how to work from within them for yourself. I include exercises and meditations to try if you want to have some felt experience to match the information to.

Chapter Three

The Personality: This Lifetime's Experience

Living from the subtle fields starts with bringing awareness to the functions of the personality. The personality of this lifetime is made up of the physical body, emotional body and mental body. The interactions between these three give us our regular, day-to-day experiences. Without input from our soul and spirit, human life is constrained by the three functions of acting, feeling and thinking. As a person drawn to reading this book, you're probably aware of more than this limited experience of life. Yet you likely started out your spiritual journey without awareness of how your personality operates. I know I did. So follow with me and recall how you used to feel. If that doesn't resonate, then relate this to others in your world. The purpose here is not to find fault with the unaware personality, but to get a feeling for the quality of life it provides.

The Unaware Personality

Our personality begins with conception and ends with death, and as such, is focused on the events of this lifetime. Life at the personality level is all about everyday aspects of people, belongings and activities. Experiences are made up of emotion, thought and action. The personality keeps very busy with the countless details of day-to-day existence. Our days are filled with clothing, feeding and caring for our bodies; transporting ourselves from place to place; fulfilling our obligations to self and others; performing the tasks of our daily work; caring for our possessions; and enjoying activities, celebrations and recreation. We live part of our lives alone and part in relationship with others. We orient ourselves to the world around us through our five senses, our thoughts and feelings.

On the personality level, we work to create a good life, whatever that means to us. Sometimes we're more successful than other times. We usually try to find a balance between what makes us feel good and what we have to do to get by. We try to orient ourselves toward positive events and away from difficult situations, but we're not always successful. Often we're very embedded with hurts and sufferings, continuously projecting old dark thoughts into current situations. We usually have immediate, habitual reactions to the stimuli of the external world. We often live with a fantasy of how we want life to be instead of noticing what's actually real. In response to life around us, we create habits that work for us both for the outside and the inside worlds. We don't really understand what life's all about, but we get on with living it anyway. In general, we're all busy trying to be the best version of ourselves we can manage.

Even though we want to orient ourselves to what makes us feel good, most of us live according to our beliefs and opinions and rarely attend to our true feelings. Our western culture has traditionally played down the role of the emotions and glorified the workings of the mind. It is only recently that we have seen images of men in tears. Being stoical is honored. The well-trained mind is sought after and revered. An educated person gains social status. People who are in touch with their emotions, who cry or otherwise express their emotions easily, have historically been perceived as weak, and passed over for prestigious positions. Babies are given alphabet blocks and other mental stimulators from birth, while being trained to control their emotions. So how are we to know what makes us feel good if we have shut down the receptors that give us the feedback? We need to know how we feel before we can figure out what makes us feel good.

Even though we over-value the human mind, it is still true that love is the human constant. We experience the importance of love at the personality level by how much our personalities yearn for it. We love love. We seek it constantly. We dramatize and glorify romantic love, familial love, patriotic love. We say we love nature, or chocolate or a certain movie. Love is the ultimate verb. Yet, living from the mind of the unaware personality, we seem to overlook the importance of love. If we have love in our lives, it's considered to be an extra, a lucky find, or a momentary high. As a culture, we don't rate love very highly in our social systems. It gets relegated to the evenings and weekends while the important business of life gets lived without it. Love is not welcome in many situations. When a young woman I know first heard about her father's fatal illness, she continued studying for an exam. When I asked her why, she replied "I feel I ought to be able to be professional about this and not let my feelings affect me." Her love and her pain were not considered professional. But without love, we hurt, and without access to our emotions, we don't know we hurt. The blind pain of this lack of love permeates our personalities and our culture.

Without the security of spirit and love in our personalities, we feel separated from everything else. We believe in our mortality and fear death. For many people, meaningful moments are very rare, and Spirit is just a concept. We often feel adrift or without purpose, and almost certainly dislike aspects of our lives. Sometimes we wonder if this is all there is to life. We're often dissatisfied or unhappy and may feel we're in a rut. To overcome this sense of lack, sometimes we fill our time with distractions, alcohol, TV, stimuli of various kinds. Other times we fill ourselves with goals or plans or events. Life feels big and incomprehensible, so we focus on small things. Parties, athletic pursuits, religious ceremonies or travel become opportunities to look for something more from life. We get involved in our kids' lives or our friends' lives and displace our lack of purpose into helping them. Hope fuels much of our pleasure. We create a vision of how we want something to be, then we paint the event with the image of our expectation rather than being alive to what is really happening in the moment. We live in a peculiar state of unawareness.

Living from the unaware personality, we feel vulnerable, and keep our guard up most of the time. Life appears as a mysterious sequence of events we have to manoeuvre through to avoid feeling afraid. To feel safe, we create controls. We manage our experience through internal rules and habits developed long ago. Often, we make the rules to protect us from feeling our true emotions. For example, a client used to be afraid to ride in cars. In her childhood her mother had a frightening accident and as a result, became very upset when the family drove together. She picked up her mother's fearful reactions and buried them deeply. As a young adult she controlled her fear by deciding she didn't like cars. She experienced them as noisy, expensive, polluting monsters. That belief worked to protect her and she rarely got in a car. After she started tuning in to her emotional body, she noticed she was inexplicably terrified whenever she was actually in a car. She realized she had created the beliefs so she didn't have to experience her fear. Bringing awareness to her beliefs and emotions created the opportunity to heal her fear and now she loves her car.

In the spiritually unaware personality, life is dominated by memories of the past, dreams of the future and opinions of the present. Little time is spent noticing what's actually happening around us and how we feel about it. We spend time worrying and wondering what might have been or what might be coming. We replay favorite scripts in our heads, passionately re-enacting scenes from our lives. In the re-enactment we can get angry, honest or funny, and say what we didn't say the first time. We build ourselves up with these fantasies. We have a certain set of thoughts and beliefs and we constantly re-affirm them. We have an opinion on everything. My boss is an idiot. That person is gorgeous. I can't do math. We don't take in information that disagrees with our pre-determined thoughts, preferring the comfort of our own beliefs, even if the belief makes us uncomfortable or unhappy. When someone insists that we hear him or her disagree with our belief, we get angry, and fight to maintain control over our own reality. We prefer the security of our illusion to the unknowns of the moment.

Our illusion becomes our reality and we hold tightly to it. For example, in my family, we were regularly asked point blank questions and then got in big trouble if we told the truth. "Who wrecked the toaster?!" No kid in their right mind was going to confess if a scene and punishment were certain. So we became good liars. Then problems began when I believed my lies. To maintain the effect of innocence, I had to believe I was innocent. The more I repeated my innocence to myself, the more real it became to me. I would get more and more vehement in my own defense until I fully believed my lie was the truth. My personality got good at reaffirming its illusions. Yet it left me feeling vulnerable. I could no longer tell what was true and what wasn't. I believed my illusion, but it felt shaky. I didn't dare question it, or I might have to face the consequences of my failings. As I brought awareness to my personality, I discovered these lies still struggling to maintain their existence with fierce denial.

The personality gets very good at hiding the shadowed parts and letting them stay hidden. Any time there are painful emotions, the personality will create a managerial program to protect the hurting self. It might agree with whatever is going on, or it might fight against it, but whatever the choice, the hurting parts get covered over but not healed. These hurting places stay hidden in the field, not feeling loved and without the joy of life. With the help of the managerial personality, they become the shadowed places deep inside, protected by denial and defenses.

Fear is a powerful force, worming its way into almost any aspect of life. Without love and awareness life feels scary, so we keep our guard up. We criticize the world as a way of staying separate from it since separation feels safe, at least in theory. Complaints come easily, and negative comments are normal. It often takes more effort to think up a nice comment than a nasty one. Good gossip dies out while bad gossip keeps circulating. But we criticize ourselves even more relentlessly than the outer world, never feeling worthy or good enough inside. We tend to feel better about ourselves when we can feel worse about someone else. We laugh at the failings of others and we're comfortable pointing the finger of blame outside while ignoring our own inner motivations.

Bringing Awareness to the Personality

Bringing awareness to the emotional and mental aspects of life is the first big step in living from the subtle fields. It brings us into the present and behind our thoughts. It makes us connect with the truth of the moment rather than an idea from the past. When we bring our attention to the fields of the personality, we become aware of how we feel, and what our thought patterns are. The awareness brings choice. How can I figure out what I'm sad about if I can't tell that I'm sad to begin with? In the unaware personality, we're often only aware of our emotions at the point when they affect our behaviour. When our contentment turns to laughter, we know we're happy. When our frustration turns to yelling, we're aware of our anger. But by becoming aware of the more subtle experience of the emotional field, we can be aware of the feeling when it first begins. Then we have a wider choice of whether or not to act, and if so, how to act. Sometimes the action might still feel appropriate; but sometimes the emotion is recognized as part of an inner reality that has nothing to do with what's going on outside, and we keep it to ourselves.

Similarly, awareness brought to the workings of the mental body reveals the patterns of our thoughts. How can we change a difficult pattern if we can't witness that it exists? A young client used to worry over whichever boyfriend she was currently involved with. She had a long drive to work and would churn through her beliefs about what was going wrong. One day she realized she had heard herself think exactly the same thought about someone else, and someone from before him too! She realized in that instant that the pattern was hers and reflected a deep habit from her childhood. By bringing awareness to her thoughts, she was able to witness what she was materializing in her world.

When we bring awareness to the workings of the personality, we can observe the choices we make of how we spend the raw material of our stream of consciousness. How do we try to make ourselves happy? Does it work? Do we blame and shame, or hide away, seek love at any cost, or block love out? Do we provoke our bosses or try to please everyone? Just what are we doing with our emotional and mental bodies all day long? To help answer these questions, let's explore how the emotional and mental bodies work, both individually and together.

The Emotional Body

The emotional body is the first subtle field beyond the physical body. It is roughly two to five inches bigger, but it varies a lot and is not uniform in thickness. Different areas can be bigger or smaller at different times. The field expands with positive emotions and contracts with negative ones. If observed from above, the outer edge of the emotional body would be irregularly shaped. Some areas would stick out further, while others would be tighter and closer to the physical body. Each chakra is capable of having a different state in the emotional body at the same time. For instance, a person who is feeling anxious might feel it in their solar plexus and throat, but not their heart chakra. Or, a person may be feeling relaxed and content over all, but if they tune in to their emotional field, they might find themselves closed off in the sacral chakra. Any combination is possible. Figure 3 is an artistic illustration of the emotional body.

The emotional body is a pretty field. It looks a bit like colored gas clouds, made up of soft pastel colors in gentle, undulating patches. The colors of the energy fields are not like the colors of the physical dimension. In the physical world, light reflects back to your eye off the surface of objects. In the nonphysical dimensions, the light is radiant, emanating from within. The colors are soft and pale, as though you were standing in a totally empty room and a colored light-bulb was turned on behind you. You wouldn't see the light reflected off any surfaces, yet there would seem to be a slight coloring in the light of the air.

Figure 3 - The Emotional Body

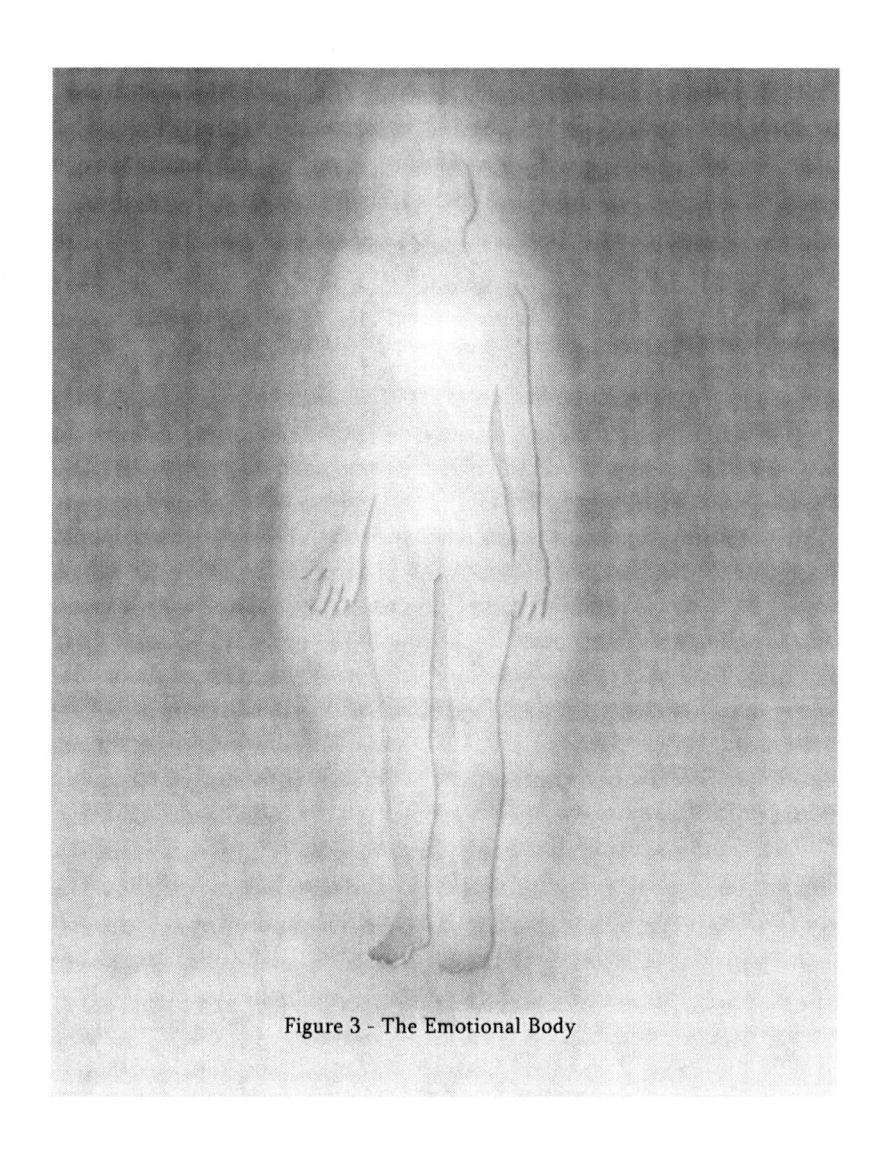

Areas of a person's emotional body that hold negative emotions or old wounds are darker, denser and closer to the physical body. They are compacted and tend not to expand and contract as easily as other areas. When something happens in the outer world that engages with these places, the person gets triggered emotionally. Then the dark place pulls in tighter, and can start a domino effect with other reactions. There is often a pain or discomfort in the physical body associated with these dark places. Most diseases and disorders of the physical body can be tracked to dense, dark patterns in the energy fields. In chapter 8, I explain how dark energy functions.

There can be a lot of motion in the emotional body. If a person is distressed, maybe feeling angry or frustrated, then the whole field can be turbulent, moving around like a balloon filled with water. If a person is very calm, maybe having just had a good meditation, his or her emotional body will be quite still.

Emotions travel within the physical body in the fluids. When we are upset, all the fluids become agitated. We cry and our eyes and noses run. We shake the fluids through sobbing or yelling, which activates the diaphragm and gets the fluids moving. Similarly, when we feel good about something, we giggle or laugh. This is also an action that gets the fluids moving. I once heard of a Hawaiian tribe that believes if a person hasn't reached the point between laughing and crying in a day, they haven't fully lived. Those people must really be in touch with the content of their emotional bodies.

Some people live a lot from their emotional bodies. These people may cry easily, laugh loudly or generally express whatever is happening in their emotional body to the outer, shared world. Their emotional bodies are large and react a lot to the stimulus from the world around. Other people choose not to pay attention to what their emotional body is doing. They hold the emotional body very close to the physical one. These people don't know how they feel about things in their lives. They often feel cut-off from their emotions, and may take refuge in analytical thought. Interestingly, those with readily available emotional bodies often have fuller, rounder figures, while those who don't connect much with their emotions are often very thin, even to the point of being bony.

Each chakra has a particular gland associated with it. The glands receive energetic impulses from the chakra when waveforms of energy vibrate through and stimulate the gland. Because the emotional body is immediately next to the physical form in density and intensity, it has large waveforms. Fluctuations in the emotional body can have an intense effect on a gland. When the gland is stimulated and releases hormones, there is an electro-chemical reaction in the body, and the person has a physical feeling associated with the emotion.

The emotional body is layered in three progressive stages. On the surface are emotions directly related to the outside world. In the middle are feelings about the self, but still in relation to the outside world. At the deepest level, the feelings are only about the self. For example, the surface might be "I'm angry at him. It's his fault. He's a jerk." This layer is all about the outside world. It deflects attention away from the hurting place by thinking only about the outer situation. The middle layer might be "I feel hurt by him. I feel embarrassed because he ignored me. I feel unimportant and uncared for by him." These are feelings about the self, but still in relation to the outside world. The deepest core level might say "I'm unlovable. I'm unworthy." There is no reference to the outer world.

In order to live in full awareness of our emotional experiences, it is important to get beneath the surface to the personal feelings. If we get stuck on the surface, our experience is all about the rest of the world and we're powerless to change anything. But if we can at least get our awareness into the middle layers about the self, then we can gain insight about our patterns and have some chance for helping ourselves. In this example, we might realize that the feeling of being unimportant and uncared for is a classic of our experience, reappearing with regularity under a wide variety of opportunities. This gives us the chance to heal the original wounds that created the feeling. Ultimately, if we can find the deepest core beliefs and bring spiritual truth to them, we can heal our deepest wounds. In Chapter 10, I cover a variety of healing options.

Practical Exercises

- *Exploring your Emotional Body*

It is possible to sit in a meditative state and feel the size, shape and nature of your emotional body. First bring your awareness to yourself as you did in the earlier chapters, sitting wherever you are, and slow down your rate of internal activity ... Feel your breath ... Now pull your awareness in behind your forehead and get connected with your central core ... Now intend to feel your emotional field and observe what you experience. Remember, all energy is conscious and connected. You can use your point of active consciousness to connect with any other energy field. Be patient and stay aware of the experience. If you expect it to happen too quickly, you'll make it up with your mind. Instead, take your time and just feel the experience happening. When working with spirit and energy, intention is the critical verb. By intending to do something, you shift your consciousness to doing it. By intending to shift to your emotional field you will do so, unless you block the activity with your mind and your beliefs. Remember that it will be a subtle feeling and one you'll need to hone yourself to be able to feel and recognize.

After reading these instructions, close your eyes and feel the nature of your emotional body. You can also use your hands to feel it around your physical form if you want. Feel how it undulates and gently waves about. Redo the exercise in which you imagine a person or activity you dislike and feel what happens to your field. It may tighten or darken or grow denser. This is less comfortable. You may have corresponding physical sensations. Now think of something you love and feel your field expand and soften. You can visit different chakras too if you like. Keep playing with it until you want to come back to the book.

* * * * * * * *

What was your experience? People usually describe their emotional bodies as feeling light, fluid or soft. If their mood is tense or uncomfortable, it might feel denser or tighter. It's possible to sense fluctuations and undulations, and it may seem to be a different size or shape in different areas. The field expands and contracts with positive and negative emotions. Sometimes it's hard to feel the emotional body of the third eye chakra. It goes against our programming to expect our thinking part to also have feelings, but it does. When we try to hold our emotions below our heads, we often end up with headaches. This type of headache usually starts across the base of the skull, behind the ears. If you experience this type of tension headache, try letting yourself open the emotional field of the third eye chakra and see if the headache softens.

Many people find their solar plexus to be tighter and less comfortable than their other chakras. We carry a lot of wounding in the solar plexus. This may be because we seek to be loved for being ourselves, but in our world, we rarely feel that way. This is especially true as children when we're creating the major patterns of our personalities. We're usually not allowed to become our own individual self. Instead, much of our behaviour is controlled by the adult world. We're told how to behave, what to do and when to do it. "Sit up straight, eat your peas, go to school" ... We aren't given the authority to manage our own sovereignty, and worse, we're judged. Since the job of the solar plexus is to house that innate sense of self, it feels bad when it isn't supported. Consequently, it feels bad a lot of the time. We often don't feel good about ourselves, feeling not good enough or unworthy at the core. These are dark feelings we house deep in the solar plexus. Consequently, the emotional field of the solar plexus is often tighter and denser than other places. All the physical disorders of the solar plexus reflect these problems. Indigestion, ulcers, hepatitis, gall stones, all are related to issues of personal sovereignty and the lack of unconditional support.

I invite you to go exploring. Bring your point of awareness inside, then go visit the emotional body in each chakra. Notice how you feel and what your regular patterns are. If you find denser, darker areas, for now you can just breath into them and watch them soften. You might want to keep track of your experiences by writing them down as you go along.

- *Feeling Emotions*

Another useful exercise is to bring your awareness to your emotional body and then induce a variety of emotions by naming them and sensing how your field responds to each one. This lets you discover exactly how your emotional field is connected to your emotions. You could try experimenting with some feelings that are similar but different, such as 'timid', 'bashful' and 'embarrassed'. Go through them one by one and really explore how your emotional field responds to each by itself. Then try another sequence such as 'happy', 'delighted' and 'ecstatic' and again see how each one feels. Then try some negative ones such as 'grumpy', 'aggravated' and 'angry' to get a sense of the differences with the darker emotions.

Every person has an emotional body and we all know what all the emotions feel like. This exercise begins to help the process of recognizing and identifying emotions. It's useful to work through a list of emotions, to learn to recognize each. It is then possible to stop in any moment in normal life to ask "How am I feeling right now?" and get some real, useful answers. There can be a wide variety of emotions active at any moment in time. Your answer might include both happy and sad, excited and nervous. Our emotional experience is rich and complex. Living fully with the emotional body in this way helps us to be grounded and realistic about the world around us. The emotional body is designed to give useful feedback. Overlooking it leaves us overly dependent on our minds.

The Mental Body

The mental body is the second field out from the physical body. In most chakras it's a little bigger than the emotional body, but in the third eye chakra it's a lot bigger since this is the location of conscious thought. Most of the mental field measures around five to eight inches from the physical body, but in the third eye chakra it can measure over two feet. The mental body is dense and structured. From the outside, it looks like a complicated grid, a dense matrix, or a lumpy, dense mesh sphere. In the third eye its surface resembles a reflective metallic cloth that shimmers. It has thicker areas that represent well-trodden beliefs, and thinner areas that are rarely accessed. The field feels hard, almost like a shell or armour. In some people it can almost seem to have sharp edges. Figure 4 is an artistic illustration of a mental body.

The job of the mental body is twofold. It both records and interprets all that is happening in our lives. First, it lays down a recording of everything that's going on around us. The entire field records what's happening in all the chakras, all the time. It stores the whole experience of our stream of consciousness, regardless of what the conscious mind is doing. Second, it records the activity of the conscious mind that interprets the incoming stimulus and makes sense of it. In the third eye we manipulate the information we have stored and establish our beliefs about what happened and why. These interpretations are then laid down throughout the whole mental body as beliefs. The beliefs create the structure or architecture of the entire mental field. In psychological terms, you can think of the third eye mental body as the conscious mind and the rest of the mental body as the sub-conscious or unconscious mind. Opening the mental body and accessing the information stored in it is like watching a movie of your own life. All the external details are there, as well as what you were thinking and feeling, and what you were coming to believe was true in the original moment.

When a person thinks with their conscious mind, it is possible to see movements of energy fluctuating through the mental body of the third eye chakra. It can look like tree roots, or lightning. One student saw tiny lights turning on and off like fireflies as thoughts raced through the mental structure. Because the physical eyes are part of the chakra, you sometimes see a person's eyes tracking with the moving currents. This is likely what Eye Movement Desensitization and Reprocessing (EMDR) is following. People store information out around their heads in a sort of short-term memory storage. The act of going to look for the stored material can be observed from the outside. In general, whenever a person brings their point of awareness to the third eye mental body, it's possible to observe them doing so. For a therapist, it becomes possible to observe if a client is still in an original story which was accessed down in a lower chakra, or if the client has moved to thinking about it in the third eye. Being in the third eye opens the possibly of creating new thoughts or false memories.

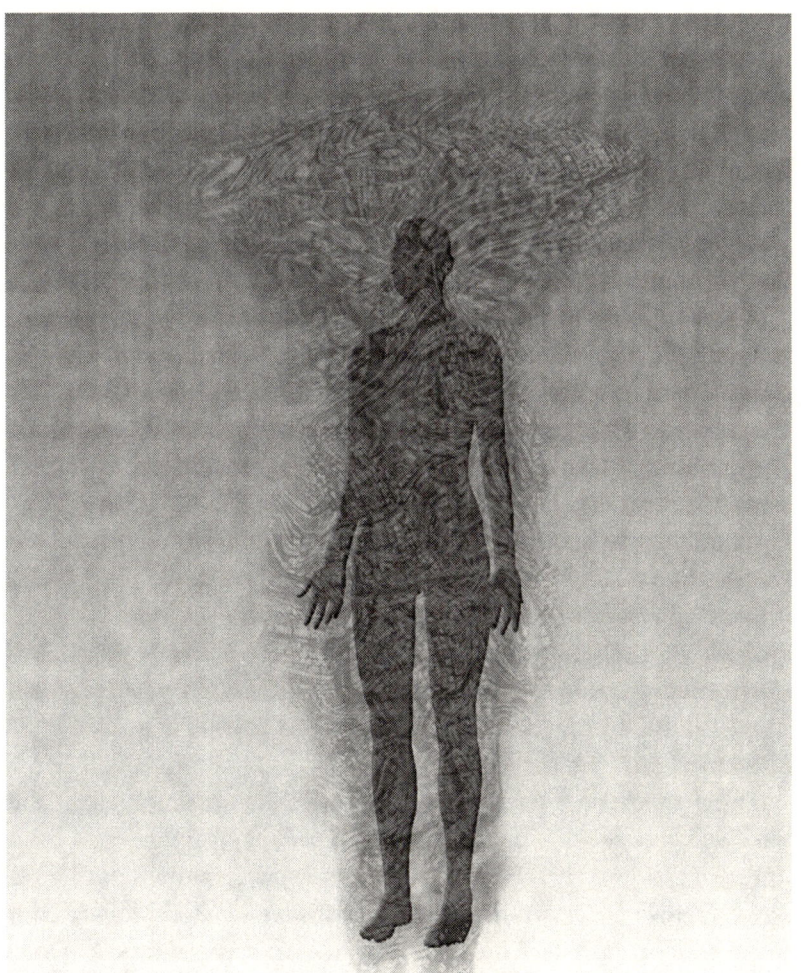

Figure 4 - The Mental Body

Some people store information in the third eye in logical ways, like a library with a system of storage retrieval. Other people store material in a haphazard way. Not surprisingly, those with the structured minds tend to do better at school, regardless of the topics that inspire them. Some clients I have worked with who suffer from Attention Deficit Disorder are not able to find their stored material at all. One man's mental body was so large he got lost in it long before he found what he was looking for. Another boy stored information in the front half of the chakra, but went out the back to go looking for it. A third woman stored information all around her whole body rather than mostly around her head.

Knowing how to find stored material is a useful human skill. I worked with a woman who was studying for a set of exams. She had studied hard, but was still very nervous about one final exam. The course covered a great deal of specific information and she was afraid she wouldn't be able to remember all she knew. I asked her to give me a list of topics she thought might be covered. Then I had her bring her awareness to her third eye mental body. When I asked her a sample question, she could feel exactly where she had stored the relevant information in her field. She was able to find the exact location out around her head somewhere, then list off all the information she had memorized there. In this way she mapped out exactly where she had stored all the information and knew she was capable of retrieving it. She scored 100% on her exam.

Some people have third eye mental bodies that are more open and flexible. These people are more 'open-minded', enjoying the experience of new ideas. Their mental bodies grow organically, and it's possible to watch them laying down new mental structures as they learn new concepts. Other people have more rigid third eye mental bodies, with distinct edges and angles. These people are more 'closed-minded'. When presented with new ideas, they return to the well-trodden pathways of their mental fields to see if the new information aligns with what they already believe. If it doesn't, they reject the new information as untrue. It's possible to observe these repeated patterns in the activity of their mental bodies.

The mental body flows through the physical body in the electrical circuitry. When I think about moving my body, I send the instructions to my limbs through the nerves and my body moves. However, unconscious beliefs that I hold in the lower chakras of my mental body can influence whether or not I'm willing to make the move. For example, if I'm trying to make myself do something I'm afraid of, say, jump into water from a height, then my third eye chakra might be sending the conscious message to jump, but my lower chakras might be refusing. This will be especially true if I have an unpleasant experience stored in the lower chakras that my active mind doesn't remember. My old belief that I will get hurt is greater than my current desire to jump. In this way our old experiences and beliefs control our current behaviour even though we may have no conscious memory of the original event. The same can be true of beliefs relating to emotional pain as well as physical pain. My head might be telling me to stay in a loving relationship, while my beliefs from sad old experiences propel me to leave. The beliefs stored in the mental body of the lower chakras may be unconscious to the mind, but they still affect our behaviour and choices.

Our behaviour can be motivated by any location in the mental body, whether we have active thought or not. We will be conscious of the reason for our actions if the motivation is coming from the third eye, and unconscious if the motivation is coming from elsewhere. If I consciously think 'it's suppertime' I can get up and go find food. This action is being led by my active mind in the third eye. It may result from a belief that there are times when I eat, or an awareness that I'm hungry. However, I can also find myself standing with the fridge door open, searching for something while thinking actively about some entirely different subject. My solar plexus is hungry and motivates my overall behaviour with the belief that there's food in the refrigerator. In this case I am acting in an 'absent-minded' way. I'm being driven to act by a lower chakra of my field. My conscious mind is literally absent from the activity, being absorbed with some other mental activity. Later, someone might ask me if I went to the fridge and I might say 'No' because I have no conscious awareness of being there. But if

I track back in my mental recording, I will in fact find the moments I stood there absent-mindedly looking for food.

It is possible to have stored beliefs in a lower chakra that dominate our behaviour, while we maintain a contradictory belief in the third eye. A woman client had an eating disorder. In her active mind, she had become very conscientious about her nutrition and diet. She was very knowledgeable and ate very well. Her third eye beliefs all supported healthy eating. However, her solar plexus held unconscious beliefs about not being in control of her own life. Whenever the unconscious beliefs were triggered by new experiences in which she felt dominated, she had bulimic episodes. Until she could access the beliefs stored in her whole field, she was unable to change her behaviour.

In order to access the stored material from earlier in life, a person must bring their point of awareness in from the mental body of the third eye, move through their energy field, and then find the relevant energy in a different chakra. Only there is it possible to engage with the mental body in the actual location where the information is stored. When the mental body gets opened, it's like re-living the stream of consciousness as it was laid down at the time of the original event. Every detail is there, even ones the individual didn't notice at the time. In healings, as clients move their point of awareness into the mental body and begin to open the relevant story, they can recall what the wallpaper looked like, what was playing on the radio or that the cat walked by the door. However, the important aspect of the stream of consciousness is what beliefs they laid down at that time. It is the beliefs that create the structure of the mental body. It is the back and forth transmissions of energy that flow between the third eye chakra and the rest of the mental body that create the embedded beliefs. It is also possible for the original story to be located in the third eye, especially if the beliefs from the story relate to feeling stupid. But the old story is still accessed by 'coming in' from the mental body and locating and accessing the energetic pattern in the chakra itself.

Practical Exercises

- *Exploring Your Mental Body*

You can explore your mental body just as you did with your emotional body. Begin with the standard action of 'coming in' ... Connect in with your body and your breath, bring your awareness to your forehead, and pull your point of awareness deep inside. Now intend for your consciousness to engage with your mental body and feel what it feels like. Use your hands to feel its contours if you can. Feel how big it is around the third eye chakra. Now let yourself go out into the third eye chakra and feel what's there. What happens when you think about something?

* * * * * * * * *

What did you feel? Most people describe the mental body as cool or cold and almost hard. It doesn't feel flexible the way the emotional body did. It feels denser, more structured and more formed than the emotional body. Sometimes it's described as almost wooden or metallic. When people access the third eye chakra, it feels like normal life. It's usually busy and full of the details of everyday life. They often forget they're practicing an exercise as they get drawn into their thoughts relating to the day. When they re-engage with the activity of exploring the mental body of the third eye, they usually laugh at just how familiar and pervasive it is!

- *Finding Memories*

Here's a fun exercise. As in the example above in which my client could find the information she studied for her exam, you can locate any memory you have stored in your third eye chakra. With this exercise, try doing it while slowly reading the directions. Try not to let your eyes jump ahead. If you know what's coming beforehand, you might interfere with it working. The first step (as always) is to come in to yourself, in behind your eyes. Then I'll prompt you to have a certain memory. As you begin to search for the memory, you will feel a tension at your forehead. Your point of awareness will go shooting out through your forehead and start scanning around like radar on a screen. Your eyes will likely start darting around. As you locate the memory, you can feel exactly where you have it stored out in your field. Your eyes and head will pull toward it. You can put your hand up into the space around your head and feel where the memory is located. As you access it you may immediately pull it into your head to process. Some people retrieve information very quickly. If so, see if you can track back out to wherever you found it. As you stay connecting with it, the memory will open more and more, and you will recall more and more of the event. You could spend an hour re-living the original experience. This is how people get stuck living from the mental body.

So begin by connecting in with yourself. Feel the vacuum strongly. Let yourself be drawn deeply inside again and get really relaxed in there.

Now, what did you eat for dinner last night?

Find the location of last night's dinner and put your hand up to it. Let yourself wander in the memories. Notice how you become able to recall more and more of the experience the longer you stay engaged with that location and memory.

Let's try the exercise again with something new. So forget about last night's dinner and pull your awareness back inside, behind your forehead and eyes again. Get really relaxed again, thinking of nothing.

Now start naming the European countries. Find the spots they're stored. They may be together in a clump, or scattered all over the pace. But for certain, they're in a different place than last night's dinner. Each different memory may be stored in a different location. You can use your hands to help identify exactly where each memory is stored.

* * * * * * * *

What did you experience? Was your hand up around your head somewhere? I do this exercise in new groups, with everyone working with their eyes closed. When almost everyone has their hand up around their heads somewhere, I have the group open their eyes. Everyone is astonished to see a room full of people with hands up in the air. Occasionally people find the exercise very difficult. This can result from a variety of reasons. Sometimes it's because they aren't comfortable leaving their active third eye. Because they can't get inside, they can't then feel what it's like to go back out. For these people, the exercise of pulling in from the mental body is very difficult. The workings of the active mind get in the way of the witness-state that's needed to observe the process at work. Reasons for staying out in the mental body vary. The person may not want to feel his or her emotions and staying in the thinking zone helps. Or they may have a belief that they're stupid, or they may have been rewarded for being smart. Then they'll cling tightly to the act of thinking in order to prove they have a good mind and can use it at any time. Or they may just be so oriented to thinking all the time that their active mind gets in the way. Persisting with the exercise always yields results.

Other people who have trouble with this exercise have such active inner critics they're certain they won't be able to do the exercise even before they begin it. The belief that they 'can't do it' dominates the experience so they actually can't. Other people find it hard to follow the instructions. Still others are just tired. If you didn't have any success, don't worry about it. Especially with the added difficulty of getting the experience through reading a book, I'm certain lots of people won't manage it the first time. But at least you know how to do it now, and can try it again any time you want. Eventually, everyone can do it easily. If you have a problem with it, see if you can figure out what's blocking you and work with the block until it releases. At the very least, you may feel this sensation of searching out around your head the next time you're trying to remember something, like a phone number or where you left your keys.

Opening the mental body of the lower chakras is more difficult and much more volatile. Without support for the potential opening of painful memories, it can be better not to start. It is very important not to re-traumatize wounded parts of the self by opening their stories and then not being able to help them. If you want to try it, begin by connecting with your Higher Self so you aren't alone and your personality isn't in charge. Get yourself into a loving condition before you ask old painful memories to show up. Then come in from the mind, drop down into a lower chakra, and begin to investigate a pattern of energy. When you enter the mental body, you will have the experience of re-living an event from your past. If it was a difficult, painful experience, please let your Higher Self help your younger self to resolve the story in a more loving way. Let the child ask the Higher Self if the scary beliefs are true.

Let the Higher energies teach the younger self directly. I believe that if we're going to open old memories, we must be prepared to help the wounded self to a happier and more loving solution, no matter what the incident is.

Unconditional support means just that: unconditional. There can be no condition in the remembered experience that would cause the adult self to judge the younger self harshly. Opening the energy means offering to help and my personal belief is that we must be sincere in this offer. The Higher Self is always ready to provide this loving assistance.

How the Emotional and Mental Bodies Work Together

The emotional body and the mental body work together like a synchronized team. Together they create the fabric of the human personality. As events happen around the physical body, the emotional body fluctuates and the mental body makes sense of it. If something significant happens, the emotional body reacts immediately. In response to its fluctuations, the mental body analyses what is happening and why. It provides beliefs to the emotional body to make sense of the experience based on previous beliefs from the past. It may also open to allow a soul-level belief to be engaged. The beliefs become the architecture of the mental field. After the event, thinking about it will stimulate the emotional body to fluctuate in the same pattern again. Thought can provoke feeling and feeling can provoke thought.

The emotional body and the mental body work together at all times. One can always trigger the other. If you have a thought about something that annoys you, the mental body is stimulated and the emotional body responds. You feel the aggravation again. Similarly, if the annoying event turns up in your life and the emotional body is stimulated, the mental body will start reacting with familiar thoughts. This is the functioning pattern of our personality level. Body, emotion and thought; all are integrated into the personal experience.

Consider an example. A happy toddler is running across the living room when she suddenly bumps into her seated dad and causes him to spill hot coffee in his lap. He leaps up, bellowing and calling for help. His emotional body will fluctuate wildly in response to the stimulus of the hot coffee. He may or may not scold her. He certainly acts in a noisy and unpredictable way. All his responses travel to the child and she receives the stimulus through her physical senses as well as all her chakras. She is likely to go into wild fluctuations as well. As her emotional body starts to react, it triggers the glands to release hormones, and she'll feel physical sensations as well. She'll probably start crying.

Meanwhile, her entire mental body lays down a recording of the event while her third eye interprets it. Her interpretation is sent to her entire mental field as an explanation for the feelings. The explanation is received as truth and the structure of her mental body is created. Let's suppose that as her emotional body feels fear, she thinks 'I'm not safe'; then her emotional body shifts to guilt, her mental body thinks 'It's my fault'; and as her emotions shift again to humiliation, her mental body says 'I'm not lovable'. These beliefs are now laid down throughout her entire mental field to explain the emotions and sensations of the event. Her third eye will be very busy during the entire episode with a lot of other thoughts as well, such as reacting to the sight of the coffee spilling or the pain of where she bumped herself. The critical beliefs though are the ones associated with fluctuations of her emotional body, and answers to the question 'why'. The beliefs create new structure in her mental body at many locations in her field. She has created a new pattern that attaches the beliefs 'I'm not safe, it's my fault, and I'm not lovable' to the emotional feelings of fear, guilt and humiliation.

This is not melodramatic. As humans, we experience these core wounds and core beliefs regularly. In every healing of a childhood wound, the client's deepest underlying beliefs are always of this nature. 'I'm bad, I'm unlovable, I'm alone, I'm not good enough, I'm unworthy.' These are the core wounds of humanity established deep in the shadowed places of our soul field, and we all have the same ones. The traumatic experience in this lifetime can be as trivial as the above example or as terrible as violent abuse. The magnitude of the cause makes some difference to the final patterning, but the process and the consequences happen regardless.

Suppose the dad goes immediately to change out of his now wet clothing. When he returns, he decides he really doesn't have time to linger over his coffee, so he leaves without talking with his daughter about the incident. Now the child's emotional body can fluctuate again with feelings of rejection and abandonment and she may feel all alone in her world. Her mental body may lay down more beliefs such as, "Daddy doesn't love me anymore. I'm on my own now". The child now has a new set of beliefs stored in her personality field that she didn't have five minutes ago. In the future, when she feels fear, guilt, and humiliation, her interpretation may be, "I'm not safe. It's my fault. I'm not lovable." When she feels rejection and abandonment, she may believe, "Daddy doesn't love me. I'm on my own."

This particular structure of the child's mental body is now available to be accessed again at any moment in her lifetime. Because the mental body records a complete moment-by-moment history of our stream of consciousness, the stored material stays there forever. Suppose a month later the girl's dad is in a bad mood over something and he scolds her roughly for a minor misdemeanor. As she feels the same fluctuations in her emotional body, she will re-use the pattern of beliefs she stored the first time and reinforce her beliefs. Through the repeated interpretations of situations, the child develops beliefs about herself and her world.

How could the father have helped his daughter not to end up holding these distressing beliefs? If he had immediately tended to her emotions and interpretations, comforting her and letting her know he wasn't blaming her and that he loved her, then she would have an immediate new set of beliefs that contradicted her original ones. She would feel loved and supported, and think 'Dad isn't scary, it's not my fault, and he loves me'. If he needed to leave the house five minutes later, all he would have to do is tell her he doesn't have time for coffee now, but he'll see her again soon when he gets back. Then her feelings of rejection and abandonment won't get established, but instead a loving explanation of why he's leaving will be available. Children will always interpret every event. It's up to their adults to help them interpret lovingly and accurately. Love heals every wound.

The emotional field is always fluctuating and the mental body is always recording all events. At important moments there are big fluctuations in emotions that result in important interpretations being recorded. The beliefs create structures in the mental field. They act as nodes in the matrix of the mental body. In this way the structure of the mental body is laid down. The mental body holds a pattern, like a bottle, and the emotional body fluctuates inside it, like fluid inside the bottle. Once the pattern has been established, it can be re-initiated, either by feeling the same sequence of feelings in a new situation, or by thinking thoughts about the original situation.

In a healing, an original story is reopened by bringing awareness to the location of distress. With the help of the spiritual Higher Self, a new set of beliefs replace the original ones. The new beliefs resonate with spiritual truth, such as 'I'm safe. I'm never alone. I'm always loved.' The new beliefs allow the person to have a different perspective on why the original event took place. But more importantly, the new beliefs create new structure in the mental body representing spiritual truth of a higher order. These new beliefs become the norm for the person, and she is able to act from a more stable and spiritually grounded perspective in her life.

Practical Exercises

- *Exploring the Mental-Emotional Interaction*

To explore the interactions of thoughts and feelings in your own field, consider a minor experience from your past that annoys you. Feel how your thoughts and beliefs trigger your emotional field to fluctuate. Now think of a delightful experience and feel how your emotions calm down again. Notice how your thoughts activate your feelings and vice versa.

It is possible to bring your awareness to this process of laying down beliefs in the moment they are happening. The skill is to observe how your emotional field is moving and to notice what thoughts you are having in response. Watch what beliefs you choose to explain a situation to yourself. This is where it's possible to get into difficulty by taking things personally if a wounded personal belief is used to explain some outer-world experience. Increasing your awareness of this process will increase your choices and you may choose less wounded beliefs to explain your world.

Chapter Four

Don't Believe Your Beliefs

One of the most difficult parts of living with full energetic awareness comes from letting go of the importance of our mental bodies and our beliefs. Because we aren't aware of the grand scheme of all life everywhere, we don't see our minds in their proper perspective and we assign them too much importance. We let our mental bodies define our reality and become very attached to our thoughts. What we think becomes what we think we are.

Recall that the job of the mental body is only to store and analyze the experience of our consciousness, it isn't to be the consciousness itself. Our thoughts are only what we're choosing to do with our consciousness in a given moment. But whatever we choose to do with our consciousness ends up becoming the material of our mental bodies. In each moment, our consciousness is doing something and our mental body is recording it. We can remember, analyze, and imagine new things relative to our recorded experiences, but we need the experience first. If we don't have a conscious experience recorded, we can't have a related thought. Our mental bodies are like libraries. If the book isn't in it, we can't access the information. This creates a lot of problems in human life that we don't acknowledge.

Many humans don't believe in spiritual or energetic phenomena. They choose to believe only in what is visible and active. They say if something isn't physical, it isn't 'real'. This creates a false starting point. Recall that when modern science measures the energy that's held in all the atoms of the universe, the amount is less than five percent of the total of all energy believed to exist. Since our personalities are aware of feelings, thoughts and dreams, let's assume the old shamans were correct, and our personalities only engage with about ten percent of all energetic reality. If the normal human world we're familiar with is only ten percent of all reality, then our mental bodies are missing a great deal of information about the nature of reality. Our libraries of recorded experience are very limited compared to what's actually available. The problem we have with our minds begins when we validate the ten percent as though it were the whole hundred percent. This is what happens in our normal human culture. We give our personalities and thoughts the importance that rightly belongs to the whole story. We mistake our limited minds for our unlimited Spirit. This is an argument of proportions. If we think 10 is 100, we'll act toward the 10 as though it were 100. We'll believe in it as though it were complete and ultimate. We'll call the rest junk.

If we need an answer to a question and we don't have relevant information, we guess. We make stuff up. We might make a lucky guess, but we're probably wrong. Without relevant information in our mental bodies, we make mistakes. We compare unfamiliar experiences to familiar ones to make sense of them. We use our own experience as a valid interpretation for things we know nothing about. Think of the humorous interpretations children give for things they've never had explained to them. We may have good intentions, but basing interpretations on what's already stored in the mental body can produce some wacky explanations.

I was once staying in an ocean-side cabin in the wilds of British Columbia with a group of people. It was peaceful and beautiful and calm. All of a sudden we were shocked by an unimaginably loud noise. We had no idea what had caused it. One person thought it was a traffic accident on the highway, a couple thought it was a bomb and one thought a cougar had jumped on the roof! We couldn't agree on what caused the noise. Yet each person held tightly to his or her own explanation and began to live in accord with it. One went looking for an accident, while those who feared bombs listened to the radio. The one who feared a cougar tried to get everyone to stay inside. It wasn't until we heard from the locals that the military were testing jets and one had broken the sound barrier that we could interpret accurately. This tiny example captures the problem we humans have with our minds. Unless the relevant information is already stored, we'll interpret incorrectly and act in accord with our interpretation.

So when it comes to spiritual phenomena, we make some really bad mistakes. First, we think the ten percent is really one hundred percent so we overlook subtle information. Second, we don't spend time and energy exploring the spiritual dimensions so we have little information to use for interpreting spiritual phenomena. We end up trying to explain nonphysical reality based on physical experiences. For example, many traditional anthropologists relate to shamanic experiences as metaphorical expressions of normal life. They don't understand that the shaman is actually accessing spiritual realms because the anthropologists have never experienced the realms themselves.

Spiritual thoughts can only be found in the mental body if there's spiritual experience to interpret. Suppose we want to know if God exists and we go to our mental bodies to find the answer. What we come up with will depend entirely on our previous experience. If we've never had a spiritual experience of any kind, there will be no relevant memory, although we may have lots of opinions. We're likely to decide that God doesn't exist. If our experience of spirit has come through listening to the leaders in our churches, mosques or temples, we'll have memories that conform to our religion. We may decide that God is something way beyond our limited scope, to be feared or revered. If our moments of personal prayer have indeed brought a deep sense of peace and well-being, we may accept that there's something bigger going on, but have no framework for understanding it. We may decide that something like God must exist but we don't know what it is. If we've also had deep personal experiences of spirit that transcend normal life and show us the inner workings of the universe, then we might decide that God is the ultimate high, to be sought in every living moment. If we've experienced complete annihilating dissolution in the Ocean of Oneness and been totally consumed by the holy fires of Divine Love, we may have a sense of the power of the mystery. We may decide that even making up the word God is a delightful expression of human earnestness. The answer we arrive at will depend completely on our previous experience. But whatever we believe, we'll accept our opinion as if it's the actual truth.

Illusion and Projection

In the unaware personality the mind is the boss and the mental body gets to determine the nature of reality. This problem of over-rating our minds gets worse when we let our thoughts define the truth about the world around us. We create a personal illusion and then accept it as real about other people and events. We believe our beliefs, even if the world tells us we're wrong.

In the normal everyday life of our personalities, we constantly receive new material through our five senses. In general we'll accept it if it's in accord with what we already believe to be true. Our beliefs grow upon each other, creating a complex reality. Usually we won't accept new information that goes against something we already believe. We block it out, choosing not to give it the credibility of truth. We reflect our own experiences and interpretations back to ourselves as though they represented objective reality. The more often we think the same thing, the more it gets patterned into the mental body and the more strongly we believe it. We think that because we believe something, that's enough to prove it's right. Our beliefs come to create the foundation of our reality, and we end up relying on our beliefs instead of our experiences to define life. We live in an illusion made up of our beliefs rather than letting life reveal itself to us.

I once moved into a house that had just been redecorated by the landlord's handyman. The landlord saw a large piece of wallpaper hanging off the wall that hadn't been trimmed properly. He asked me why I had re-papered when his man had just finished the job. I replied that I hadn't done any re-papering; that the wall had been like that when I moved in. He replied sternly, "No. You must have re-papered because my man wouldn't have left a job like that." He maintained his incorrect belief that I had re-papered forever, even asking me once why I had chosen that particular wallpaper since it was the same as he had in his other properties. He even thought I had picked the same pattern he picked. His opinion about his handyman defined his truth about my wall. His actual experience of the wall and of my reality were ignored.

The problem with believing our beliefs is how we then use them to create reality. We manifest the world around us based on our opinions and beliefs. If I believe the Earth is flat, I won't take my boat very far from shore. Beliefs limit experience. If I believe my mother didn't love me, I'll never feel her love. Beliefs limit intimacy. If I believe I shouldn't get too big for my britches, I'll never discover what I'm capable of. Beliefs limit expression. If I believe a country is my enemy, I'll create conflict with them. Beliefs create outcomes. Whatever I choose to include in my mental storage tanks, those beliefs become my reality, and I make them matter, for myself individually, and for all life as a collective.

But what is a belief? It's only an old thought I had at some point in the past that seemed to make sense in the moment. It's nothing more than that. It may not have been true then, or it may have been true back then, but is no longer true now.

This is how we create illusion. The mental body is the great storehouse of the whole illusion of life. It surrounds our body with a dense mesh of interpretations and explanations and houses a whole lifetime of memories. We look out through it to the world around us and, like a veil, it clouds our perception. Observing through this veil, we then superimpose our reality onto the stimulus that comes from outside. We perceive external events according to our illusion. First we interpret the events according to what we already believe. Then we predict what will happen next. We begin to believe that we know how and why things are happening. We believe our beliefs about the outside world. And since we are staunchly committed to believing our beliefs are the truth, we rarely change our minds about something.

A real problem of living in the illusion begins when we apply our mental reality to other people. We project our interpretation onto them, whether it fits or not. At the personality level, we willingly interpret other peoples' lives. We think we know why people do things. We use our personal 'truth' to explain someone else's behaviour. We mistakenly assume our reality is an accurate interpretation for someone else. But it can't be. Our interpretation of another person's behaviour is a reflection of our history and not theirs. At the personality level, within the mental body, our experience can't be about anyone else; it can only be our own. Every time we believe we know why a person did something, it's a projection of our reality onto them. We're almost certain to be wrong. We can only know the reasons for our own choices, and we don't usually even know them! All we can know about another person is what words and actions they choose to materialize in their outer world and our experience and interpretation of them. Whenever we apply our perspective to someone else, we mirror our own reality back to ourselves through our interpretation. Even with our intimate family and friends all we really know is our interpretation of what they have chosen to share with us. We still have no real idea what their inner reality is like. We aren't privy to how they spend their stream of consciousness.

Suppose a group of people are sitting together in a room and one of them begins to sneeze uncontrollably. If we asked each person why the other was sneezing, we'd hear a variety of answers. The person with a cat allergy would think it had to do with allergies. The person trying to avoid getting a cold would think it was a virus. The person with environmental sensitivities would think it was from the glue in the rug.

Each person would explain the unknown based on his or her own personal experience. As a suggestion, that's fine. But the problem is that people usually believe their own interpretations about life. If asked to respond to the sneezer, one would offer allergy medicine, one would leave the room and one would complain to the building owner about the carpet. In the unaware personality, people don't stop to question their own interpretations. Instead they project them onto the world around and act as though their thoughts are valid.

We do this collectively as well as individually. Our culture represents the total of all our joint beliefs. We may not agree on the content of our illusions, but we agree that the illusion itself is real. We carry our collective history with us wherever we go and we think about it over and over. In a universe where nothing is ever the same from one moment to the next, we choose to create static beliefs. Then we cling to the versions of reality created by them.

Why we Believe our Beliefs

So why do we live through our beliefs so totally? It's as though we're collectively addicted to thinking. We lose ourselves in the mental fabric and never go looking to retrieve ourselves. What makes the mental body so attractive? The reasons are varied. They include the intensity of the personality level, the status of thinking, the importance of self-identity and the role of fears.

The first reason for believing in our beliefs is the intensity of the dense dimensions. The experiences of the personality level are very demanding and it's easy to get completely caught up in them. The ten percent of life we're familiar with is very local and very intense. It's dramatic and exciting. It involves our bodies and our senses. It commands our attention and we get mesmerized by its attraction. We get drawn out into the mental body easily because the experience is so compelling. It seems so believable! Compared to the nebulous subtle experiences of spirit, it just feels so much more 'real'. It keeps us busy and leaves us with little opportunity to feel what else is happening. That's why the spiritual journey always begins with meditation in which the mind is quieted and the subtle feelings become recognizable. Without meditation, the ever-active mind remains the dominant experience of life.

The second reason for over-rating our beliefs is the status we give to thinking. The mind is what separates us from the rest of the animal kingdom. We're the planetary experts in thinking. As a species, we've specialized in using our mental bodies. Analysis is recognized as one of the great human accomplishments. We revere thinking and glorify the great thinkers of our times. Education and intellect are ranked highly in our social schemes. To prove to others that we're worthy of respect, we have to show how good we are at thinking. People sometimes get themselves locked out in their mental bodies for exactly this reason. They can't experience spirit for fear they won't appear 'smart'. This is especially true for people whose parents cared a lot about schooling and grades. Anything but thinking is considered as 'less than'. In our world of hierarchies and judgments, we aren't willing to give up something we've gained status for, so we don't want to give up the importance of the mind. Who would we be without the status thinking gives us? Who would we be if we related to thinking as nothing more than a tool of the spirit?

A third reason for our commitment to our beliefs is the importance of our thoughts in our self-identity. Our collective belief is that we are what we think we are. We identify deeply with our opinions. Imagine a group of people at a meeting. Each person has ideas. The ideas become an extension of the person. Many people are so attached to their ideas they won't give them up or accept someone else's instead of their own. The idea becomes part of the person's self-identity. If someone doesn't like our idea, we feel as though they don't like us and we react emotionally. We let our ideas and beliefs define who we think we are. When a person has an opinion they're attached to, they work hard to convince other people to believe it too. They'll fight to get others to agree with them. If the other people do agree, the person feels secure in believing their belief is the truth, and they feel good about themselves. If the others don't agree, the person feels vulnerable and defensive.

People collude with each other in this manner every day. Suppose a friend is trying to get you to agree with him about something that doesn't really matter to you at all. You're most likely to hop on the bandwagon and agree anyway, just in order to help him feel good about himself. However, suppose he's trying to get you to agree with something you have a strongly different opinion about. Then you're likely willing to get into conflict to keep your own truth secure. If you accept his opinion, it feels like you're giving a piece of yourself away. This reflects the attachment of self-identity to our thoughts and opinions. We feel disempowered when we bow down to someone else's opinions instead of holding true to our own.

It seems that this disempowerment and consequent attachment to the illusory self comes in large part from our style of child-raising. Children are given little power in decisions that affect their lives. The structures of family and society don't usually respect the child's sovereign domain. Adults don't tend to say "Show me who you really are. Reveal to me your best self so I can help you become it." Instead, as children we live surrounded by people who want to remake us according to some plan. We're told how to dress, how to behave, what to do and not do with our lives. "Smile for Mrs. So-and-So, go to school, eat your beets, be quiet ..." We end up losing our sovereign identity in the wrangling for a bit of self-determination on the personality levels. We work both with and against all the influences of parents, peers, school and media to create a sense of personal self. Consequently, we don't want to give up this hard-earned self-concept. Whatever beliefs go with this personal self, we want those thoughts to stay. Giving it up feels like abandoning the inner children who worked so hard to create it. To honor our own challenges and growth, we staunchly defend our choices. This keeps us firmly attached to our illusions and projections.

A final reason for believing our beliefs is related to the level of fear we live with on the personality levels. In the ten percent reality, love is often lacking. Without love, life can be dark and frightening and we feel isolated and vulnerable. Whenever anything hurtful happens, we create new thoughts to try to protect us from it ever happening again. Our important beliefs are often laid down at times of distress. We feel fearful until we have some idea that helps us to feel better. Because it helped in that moment, it gets a lot of validity in our inner schemes. We tend to think it often. We feel the belief itself will protect us. For example, a child who is humiliated by an adult for asking a penetrating question may decide that her questions are stupid. As life progresses, the child may become an individual who never asks questions because she thinks she'll be judged for needing to ask. She protects herself from humiliation by believing her questions are stupid. The belief becomes the protection.

Since fear has a lot of power in the personality levels, when we think about giving up the authority of the mental body, we immediately feel afraid. Who will protect us if the mental body isn't allowed to? Without our beliefs we feel defenseless. We also fear who we'll be if we aren't who we think we are. The idea of surrendering the hard-won self to an unknown is terrifying. We fear being vulnerable and open to attack, being judged and ridiculed. We fear change and not being in control; we fear loss, and things getting worse. We're afraid that people who love us won't love us if we change, or that we won't love them. We fear not fitting in, not being 'normal', or being rejected and abandoned. We fear that we won't know ourselves, or we'll cease to exist. These fears and many others loom up and limit us whenever we think about breaking out of the prison of our illusion. The fears keep us attached to believing our beliefs.

So we control our environment to avoid feeling our fear. We try to build a static life that's familiar and safe. We feel comfortable if we think we know what's going on and can control our reality. But we feel very vulnerable to being hurt if we're not in control. Other people might take advantage of us, or we might make fools of ourselves. So we create the illusion that we know what's going on to give ourselves confidence on the inside. The illusion is maintained by outlawing any thoughts that don't accept the current belief structure as the truth. This familiarity with thought patterns allows us to feel safe from anticipated outcomes. We avoid feeling vulnerable by maintaining that our illusion is real.

The fears originated in experiences long ago, but as part of the mental body the fears become structures of the illusion itself. We create the very things we're afraid of in our experiences and interpretations. The mental body does its work by storing the fears and vulnerabilities each time we revisit them. This means the need to be afraid is also part of the illusion. Ask yourself when the last time was you were physically attacked by someone. The answer is probably measured in years, if ever. Now ask when the last time was you were emotionally or verbally attacked by someone. The answer is probably measured in a smaller number of years, or months. Now ask when the last time was you attacked yourself. The answer is probably measured in minutes. You see, we've locked ourselves inside with the bad guys, believing in our fears, and projecting our beliefs onto the outside world. We create our own familiar thoughts to protect us from our own familiar fears. The entire drama lives in the illusion of our mental bodies and we project it out onto the world around us. In the reality of any moment, the thing we're afraid of almost certainly doesn't exist. It may have existed at a time in the past, but it most likely doesn't exist in this moment, except in our minds. If you examine fears closely, you'll find that the bulk of them relate to possible future experiences. Not only are they in the future and not a current event, but they aren't even very likely to happen. They are only possibilities.

So we spend a huge amount of our stream of consciousness worrying over unlikely future possibilities, based on long-ago scary moments. Since the worrying feels like it's warding off the possibility of attack, we spend a lot of time doing it. We get attached to thinking about the fear of attack and the protection of our defense strategies.

So the problem we've created with our limited mental bodies is that we over-rate our minds, believing in our beliefs, and fearing to let go of them. We identify with the illusion we've created in the ten percent world and we're afraid to look any further. The solution to this problem is to stop believing so strongly in the illusion and to find out what else exists. What's in the other ninety percent? How can it help to create a good life?

As a person moves toward a spiritually oriented reality, the mind stops being glorified. For a period of time the mind may be seen as a hindrance or a foe. But ultimately the mind takes its place as a servant of the spirit. The importance we assign the personal mind gets surrendered little by little. When a person comes to know himself as spirit, his self-identity dissolves into his awareness. Opinions come and go. They represent nothing more than the moment. On the path of enlightenment, we come to live without opinions. There's a great relief in not having to be right all the time, in not needing to know everything. It's a relief to have something greater to follow than just the old thoughts we've accumulated along the way. As we expand, there's so much more available, that the mental body comes to take its appropriate place in the big picture. It is a wonderful tool of the spirit, but it needs to be the servant, not the boss.

Chapter Five

The Soul Level: Past Lives and the Collective Unconscious

It seems our physical body is the vehicle for our Spirit's journey as we explore what's humanly possible over a long timeframe. This journey can be thought of as an individual or a collective action, as a progression of individual past-lives or as collective human history. Either way, it lasts over countless lifetimes. We're like a great tree growing in a forest. Every year the tree sprouts new leaves as it experiences another season of growth. The storms and sunny days come and go, bending and shaping the ever-growing branches. Eventually the leaves lose their vitality and die, but the tree remains. Our lifetimes are like the seasons of the leaves. We grow a new body for this season's learning. Yet the great tree of human wisdom grows from lifetime to lifetime. It would be foolish for a leaf to think there was no tree, just as it would be foolish for a human to think there was no ongoing soul.

The storehouse of all this past experience is the soul dimension of the energy fields, also known as the collective unconscious. It is an intermediate zone, between the spirit dimensions and the personality level. In an adult, the soul field measures about three to five feet across, ending approximately arms-length from the body. The energy feels similar to that of the personality level, but the texture is finer. If the personality fields are like homespun cloth, the soul field is more like finely spun linen. Chakras seven, eight and nine are in the soul level. Seven is the crown chakra through which the higher energies are anchored into the soul. Eight is the relational, extroverted chakra through which soul-level relationships are felt. Chakra nine is the personalized, internal soul experience. Figure 5 is an artistic impression of what a soul field looks like.

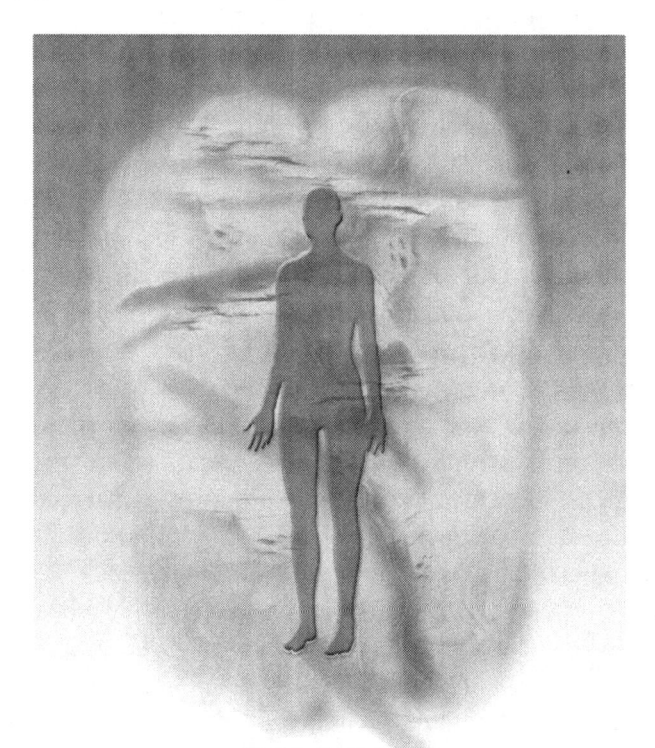

Figure 5 - The Soul Field

Whenever spirit energy takes form in the physical dimension it must come through the soul level to do so. If Spirit wants to experience life as a dog, it comes in through the dog soul field. If it wants to be a pine tree, it comes through the pine soul, known as its deva. The soul experience includes the collective history of the species on the planet as well as the specific configurations of the individual soul. The planet is teeming with intermingling soul fields of all different forms and styles. Perhaps these collective soul fields make up the 'dark matter' science has discovered. The dark matter is nonphysical and invisible, but can be 'seen' by its effect. It exerts a force field on physical forms, helping them to keep their shape and stay together. This is very much what the purpose of the soul field looks like in its physical effects. Each incarnation has a new body and personality for the soul and spirit to grow through. The soul houses ongoing explorations and incomplete understandings. It determines what our core outlook on life is and what our disposition is. It provides our tendencies and talents.

Our current incarnation is neither more nor less important than any other incarnation of the journey. In each lifetime we live fully, learning about love and the absence of love, about how to treat people and how it feels to be treated in various ways. We learn what is possible, and ultimately what is wise. We take different risks and undertake different projects. From lifetime to lifetime, we grow and adapt, eventually becoming wiser and more sophisticated as we incorporate more understanding of love into our daily existence.

This model of human life is as old as human understanding. It is recorded in the writings of many ancient traditions, including the Egyptian Book of the Dead and the Tibetan Book of the Dead. These traditions speak of two souls, or two drops, one inside the other. One soul ends with this mortal death while the other, indestructible one goes on eternally until reunion with God. The everlasting one determines the mood, or disposition of the person. The disposable one develops during a lifetime, but ends with death. In Tibetan Buddhism and other spiritual traditions, certain children are recognized as the reincarnated souls of previous spiritual teachers. Because the culture makes use of reincarnation, these people don't need to re-establish themselves as important teachers in each lifetime, but can be given the opportunity to go on with their explorations without hindrance. Wouldn't it be a different world if we all knew who we had been before? Are there great souls of the past that are incarnate again now? Is Mozart among us? Or Einstein? These may be reasonable questions to ask.

Perceiving the Soul Field

The soul field is not physical as there are no atoms or molecules present. Instead, it is etheric. Etheric energies are quite dense and fairly easy to learn to perceive. They look like patterns of light. Souls can be seen whether they have created their physical form yet or not. Before incarnating, the soul appears as a starry cloud of light energy, referred to as a 'soul star'. After conception, as the soul incarnates, the soul field expands as the physical, emotional and mental bodies grow within it. Ultimately, the soul field remains larger and more expanded than the personality level, with the smaller fields nested within it. There is also an etheric template stored in the soul level that is used as the blueprint for building the physical body. This template looks like a highly complex pattern of coded light, like a light body, which is exactly what it is. In the movie Revolution, the final movie of The Matrix trilogy, the opening sequence comes very close to rendering graphically what the etheric template actually looks like. Once the physical body has formed, the light from the etheric template can be seen as a haze of white light emanating beyond the skin. It looks like a thin white haze surrounding the person, only an inch or two thick.

The experience of the soul level is similar to that of the personality. There is an integrated emotional-mental function that is structured with beliefs and habits. When a person has an experience that triggers a soul level emotional response, then soul level beliefs are also engaged. Some of these are wise, but some are very dark. The dark, wounded beliefs are those deeply held core beliefs that may not make sense from this lifetime. These are the subtle underlying beliefs that seem to define reality even when all understanding points to a better option. Core beliefs of this kind include unworthiness, feeling bad or unlovable, hating ourselves, deep shame and guilt, or deeply held fears of certain types of people or situations. Beliefs from traumatic death experiences, rapes, tortures, burnings or other terrifying acts we know both as victim and perpetrator are locked away in our souls. We feel shame and self-hatred for participating in hurtful acts and we fear being hurt again. Whatever energetic patterns exist in the soul dimension, the incoming human carries the effects. As soon as an opportunity arises in the new lifetime, the old beliefs get re-established. As we saw in our example of the child spilling her Dad's coffee, she accessed old beliefs of being unsafe, being at fault and being unlovable to make sense of her frightening experience. These beliefs would have originated in her soul field.

Reincarnation and the Etheric Template

When a soul wants to incarnate, the soul star hangs around in the fields of its intended parents. Some native traditions believe the incoming soul appears in a dream to the parents, asking permission to be born to them. If the parents agree, a spiritual contract is entered into by all parties. In our western, logical tradition, we have no awareness of the incoming soul appearing in a dream, but it may still happen. But with or without the dream, it seems there is an agreement between the parents and the soul to have the family experience. In fact, it seems to work as good birth control to be in a firm 'No' on the soul level. Sometimes parents who want to conceive are unable to because of old beliefs being held in the soul field. Once these beliefs are cleared and the parents become welcoming in their souls, then conception can happen more easily.

It's possible to see the soul star in the mother's field and sometimes also in the father's field before conception. It's also possible to connect directly with the soul star and sense the nature of the incoming person. It seems that some souls want a male life, some want a female life, and for some, it seems not to matter. So there can be two different souls hanging around together, waiting to see if the fertilized ovum is male or female before one descends and the other vanishes, at least for the time being. It may well return when the couple is considering conceiving another child.

At the time of conception the soul moves down right in front of the woman's belly and a great shaft of white light can be seen going directly into her womb. Although ovum and sperm may have already met and the process of cell division begun, it's only when the soul engages with the process that conception occurs. Without the soul engaging, the cells will pass right through the mother's body. This is why in vitro fertilization can be so tricky. The cell division may have taken place in the laboratory, but if the incoming soul doesn't engage with the process, the fertilized ovum will pass through the mother's womb. I remember feeling the moment of soul engagement in my own pregnancies as the moment when I suddenly 'knew' I was pregnant. I could feel the arrival of another person engaging deeply in my body and my energy field. I have also had the incredible honor of witnessing the moment of energetic conception a number of times in the healing room, both naturally and through helping the incoming souls to engage after an in vitro intervention. As the soul engages with the physical dimension, the etheric template begins to operate in the uterus and the soul begins the tricky business of building its new body according to its blueprint.

Researchers have discovered how to photograph the etheric template of growing plant leaves using Kirlian photography.[12] As a bud forms, a pattern of light comes into existence in the shape of the fully formed leaf. The plant borrows molecules from the earth to fill up the pattern and the leaf slowly materializes in accord with its blueprint. The etheric template is held in the soul or devic level of the plant. This etheric template can also be witnessed by looking at the aura field of a tree in the spring. Even though the tree has only buds on its branches, the aura will be the shape of the tree when it is in full leaf.

Exactly the same thing happens with humans. After conception, it is the work of the etheric blueprint to guide the growth of the body. Molecules are attracted to fill up the requirements of the pattern.

The incoming soul uses the parents' DNA for raw material. It turns the DNA on and off according to its own plan laid down in the codes of its etheric template. The coding of the light body is the DNA. The template is highly sophisticated and complex. Its intention is to guide the growth of a very complicated organism. It is because the etheric template exists that a molecule knows whether to become part of a fingernail or a kidney cell. However, quite often the growth process goes awry and the embryo has to abort its attempt. This is reflected in the high rates of early miscarriage. Medical science suggests that possibly seventy-five percent of conceptions do not proceed to live births but stop before the nine months are complete.[13] In some cases it seems to be because the complicated growth process is not going well. In other cases, it seems that the soul has had enough of the physical environment after a few days or weeks to fulfill its purpose, and chooses to move out again.

In my own experience, I was blessed with easy pregnancies with my first four children, but had an early miscarriage with my last child. I could tell I was pregnant, but I felt dreadful. I was green with nausea, and had pain in my uterus. I felt weak when I stood up, and couldn't imagine what a whole nine months would be like. After ten days or so, the baby miscarried, and it was a great relief to my body. The very next month the same soul energy was back and grew easily and comfortably. When my son was young he said he was aware of trying once before managing to make it in to the physical dimension successfully.

Because the etheric blueprint exists on the soul level, it reflects the state of the body during past lifetimes. If there was a bad physical trauma, the template will still hold the memory of it. The memory may cause a physical weakness that can be passed along from lifetime to lifetime. Birth defects can be accounted for by one of two things. Either the growth process didn't go smoothly, and somehow the intentions of the blueprint weren't carried out correctly, or the disorder existed in the blueprint and is being re-initiated in this lifetime, maybe for additional exploration or for healing.

Traumatic death experiences are frequently recorded in the etheric template. For example, a client suffered from extreme asthma from the day she was born. When we opened the energy of the asthma, it took us to a previous lifetime where she was a woman in a forest at night, running for her life. A group of men were chasing her. She ran on and on, her breath ragged and burning. As she was gasping for breath, the men caught up with her and ran her through with a sword from behind. As she died, her lungs burned with pain, her emotions convulsed with terror and shame, and she laid down the beliefs that men could deprive her of her life and she didn't deserve to live. As soon as she was initiated into this lifetime through the birth process, she re-initiated these conditions. She had suffered from asthma her whole life and had a rocky relationship with her father that gave him ultimate authority in her life. Through the healing process, she cleared the energies, transformed her relationship with her father, and her asthma improved dramatically.

Whether the traumatic death was from a recent lifetime or from long ago, I don't know. It could be that her soul has lived a number of lives with severe asthma, or it could be that she chose to turn the DNA on to elicit the asthma in this lifetime alone. Since the etheric template is part of the soul, and the soul is guided by Spirit, it is possible for the soul to choose to explore an aspect of life in one lifetime but not others. The woman may have chosen asthma in this lifetime in order to help heal her intense fear of men. Or it could be that the story and energetic pattern existed as part of a collective human history and the woman initiated it to clear it from the human soul field. Any reasoning is possible. In general, it seems we turn the DNA on and off to elicit certain lessons and options in different lifetimes.

The existence of the soul dimension and the etheric template can explain evolution and inter-generational learning. Researchers have trouble explaining why second or third generation animals know a certain bit of information that was taught to their ancestors, but not to them. If the animal is the reincarnation of the earlier soul, the learning is already stored in its field.

A few years ago I had a wonderful kitten named Molly. She came to us from a farm and was a fearless explorer. I was always afraid she would be hit by a car since she seemed to have no awareness whatsoever that cars were dangerous to her. We kept her indoors for the first year of her life, but eventually decided to let her out. My old male cat Kea, who is terrified of cars, kept trying to nudge her away from the road. Within a week my fears were validated when she was killed by a car. My first thought after the trauma of discovery and response was that in her next lifetime, she would be afraid of cars. I thought that Kea must have been killed by a car in a previous life to have such an ingrained response to them. A few years later it seemed that Molly came back to us, recognizable in both her soul and her physical characteristics. She is now a determined housecat, running away from the open door to the street instead of ever wanting to venture out. If she is indeed a reincarnation of the first Molly, it's certainly possible that her soul 'remembers' what happened the last time she went out that door. This process of learning and reincarnating can explain much of the process of evolution.

Identical Twins

One of the most fascinating facts about souls is that identical twins have only one soul field. Identical twins are a single soul that has chosen to incarnate through two personalities. Similarly for any multiple births, if the individuals are identical, they all originate from one soul. It's possible to see the large soul field with the individual personalities and bodies within it. Because the soul holds the etheric template for the physical body and makes decisions about turning the DNA on and off, the result is the same for all the growing bodies. Hence they are identical.

Having one soul explains why twins have such similar tastes and desires, and why they seem to have an uncanny awareness of the other. Since the eyes are the gateway to the soul, looking into the eyes of identical twins feels like looking at only one soul. I once had the honor and pleasure of working with identical twin adult women who were very willing to share their experiences with me. These women had similar core beliefs, fears and expectations about life. They dreamed the same dreams at night as well. In meditation we were able to access the reason why they had chosen to come as two rather than one. They were aware that loneliness had been a debilitating problem in previous lifetimes, and if they came as two beings, there would always be the other one to commune with. Although they lived in different cities, the sisters talked by phone every day.

Scientific inquiry into human development has long been fascinated with the question of nature versus nurture. Which is more important to human development, the nature the person was born with or the nurturing he or she received in childhood? In relation to the energy fields, this question can be restated as, which is more important to human development, the soul or the personality? To study this question, researchers located sets of identical twins who had been separated at birth and raised in different parts of the world. It was assumed the twins would have the same nature since they had the same DNA and physical form, but since they had been raised in different homes and even in some cases in different countries, the nurturing process would be totally different. The adult twins were brought together and measured using a wide array of psychological tests. They had uncanny similarities in many unusual and unexpected ways. For example, one pair of men wore identical clothes, had the same highly eccentric belt-buckles and both enjoyed surprising people by singing in elevators![14]

The final summary result of the nature versus nurture studies is that the ratio of nature to nurture appears to be roughly 50/50. That is, nature accounts for half of our make-up and nurture for the other half. This suggests that our soul experience accounts for half our make-up, while this lifetime's personality accounts for the other half. This makes sense to me. It somehow feels comforting to know that I can rely on half of my inner world to be familiar. I can imagine saying yes to the challenges of another lifetime if I'd be familiar with roughly half of what transpires.

Healing with the Etheric Template

Since the etheric template holds the pattern for the physical body, it can be accessed to help with physical healing. Suppose a person has an accident and suffers an injury to his body. He would likely have an emotional reaction to the event such as fear or anger experienced in the emotional body. This reaction would cause the emotional body to fluctuate in the area of the injury and the fluids in his physical body would swell. He would also have thoughts that occurred during the accident that would be stored in his mental body at the location of the injury. This mental aspect would affect the nerves of the injured area, causing elevated pain.

It is possible to speed healing of the injury by engaging purposefully with the energy fields. The person would first bring his awareness into the injury, exploring both the emotional and mental memory stored in the tissues. Through this process, the emotions could be cleared and the fluids calmed down. The beliefs could also be relaxed from the mental body through bringing awareness to them, connecting with the higher energies and finding out if the beliefs were valid or not. At the point when all that was left was the damaged flesh, it would be possible to access the etheric template and reactivate it in the physical body to speed the physical healing. In essence, it's like reminding the cells of the state they were in before the trauma. Using the template accesses the original pattern for the cells in that part of the body and reminds the regenerating tissue of its blueprint. Miraculous healings happen within very short time periods when this technique is employed.

One day I was hiking with a friend. Climbing a steep embankment I gouged the front of my thigh badly on a root hidden in the mud. There was a nasty welt with a deep scratch about six inches long. When we arrived back at my friend's house, I proceeded to do healing work on my leg. In entering into the emotional memory, I recalled the shock and extreme fear of falling I had experienced in the first moments, before my friend had turned around to help me. I also recalled my embarrassment and chagrin at needing the help. From the mental field I realized my first thought had been that I was going to fall down the cliff and suffer serious injury. However, as my friend turned to help, my thoughts shifted to worrying that I would hold him up from continuing the hike. In revisiting the story I realized I hadn't fallen, we had completed the hike, and my friend hadn't minded at all. After I had cleared the emotional and mental bodies through re-visiting them in this loving way, I then reactivated the etheric template. All this involved was the awareness of the etheric template existing in my leg and a conscious intention to reconnect the torn tissue with it.

I had worked my way along about half of the wound with this technique when I was called to supper and I didn't return to my healing. The next day the wound was remarkable. The lower half on which I had worked had no pain, no bruising at all, and only a thin scratch with a dry scab. The half I had not worked on was very sore, deeply bruised and had a thick, nasty scab. While the part I worked on was completely healed within a couple of days, the upper half took over two weeks before the deep bruising was completely gone.

In cases where the etheric template itself is holding the weak pattern from an earlier life experience, it is also possible to heal the template itself. We brought about such a healing for my client who had the debilitating asthma. In the healing we first cleared all the emotional issues and beliefs the woman had established during the death experience that came while being chased through the forest. Once the soul level emotional and mental fields were both clear and stable, we accessed the etheric template for her lungs as they had existed in that earlier lifetime, from before the men started chasing her. We then re-established the original healthy template in the lungs of both the original body and her current body. This allowed the cells of her body to begin realigning with a new pattern that did not involve gasping for air. This technique heals the current physical body as well as healing the etheric template itself. The weak condition need never reoccur.

Karma

Karma is the natural law of consequences, playing out at the soul level. This natural law functions in the soul just as it does in the personality. In the personality level, if you harm someone, your relationship bears the consequences of your actions until you make proper amends. Suppose you habitually lie to a friend who trusts you. When the friend finds out about your deceit she'll stop trusting you. This is a natural consequence of your choices. The new condition of distrust lasts until you make serious amends to change it. If you take full responsibility for your actions, sincerely apologize, explain what led you to such untrustworthy behaviour, and if you heal your underlying wounds that caused your lying, your friend might consider trusting you again. But she'll probably only trust you again through observing that your new behaviour is actually trustworthy. You bear the consequences of your actions until you learn your lessons and sincerely change your behaviour.

The same law of consequences occurs in the soul levels. Depending on the quality of your soul level interactions with people, you will carry forward consequences to subsequent lifetimes until you have learned and changed. Take driving as an example. If you occasionally cut people off on the road because of oversight or mistake, you don't accumulate karma. However, if you habitually swerve around people and cut them off so your habit reflects your intentions and choices, this does create karma. You purposefully or callously endanger strangers. This karma would probably be worked out in relation to your interactions with strangers and your remorse about harming a stranger in a mild way. The consequence fits the situation. However, if your aggressive driving causes another person to have a serious accident, you are now in a karmic relationship with that soul. Your actions created a consequence that affected the soul journey of someone else. You will bear the consequences of that action on a soul level until you learn and change.

The healing need not involve the exact soul from the experience. The collective unconscious is far more complex than that. But the healing still needs to happen relating to your inter-dependence with strangers. As you learn and transform, you naturally right the imbalance in the collective soul field that you first created. In this way, you can clear your own karmic patterns whether or not the other soul is also healing. The victim of the car accident can learn forgiveness whether or not the aggressive driver has healed his wounds. Similarly, the aggressive driver can realize the error of his ways and heal and be forgiven by spirit whether or not the injured stranger attends to his own feelings of victimization.

Karmic patterns can connect us to specific individuals. Again, they operate in the same way as personality level patterns do between people. On the personality level, suppose you loaned a friend a large amount of money and he never repaid you. Or maybe it was the other way around and you were the borrower who hadn't repaid the debt. There will be energy between the two of you that reflects this situation. If you run into each other at the grocery store, your interaction will be strained. If you know the other one is invited to a dinner party, you might decline your invitation. Until the energy of the financial debt has been settled, the relationship between you is affected and you aren't free to move on to other things together.

For a relationship to be affected, it doesn't need to involve a debt. It could be related to anything. Suppose that all the way through high school there was a person you disliked intensely, and sometimes your dislike caused you to be unkind to them. For whatever inner reasons of your own, you believed things about the person that triggered you, and you chose to act out your negative emotions in your relationship with them. Now if you run into this person in your adult years, the energy between you is not clear. The old patterns surface again and have to be dealt with. If you take responsibility for your earlier actions, you can change the energy with the person. You might apologize, or invite them for a meal or a coffee, or some other kind act. In this way you begin to right the wrong you committed earlier and the consequences shift. Your energetic relationship with the person changes.

Exactly the same thing happens on the soul levels with souls we have engaged with before. If you had a good or difficult relationship with a particular soul in some previous lifetime, and you cross paths with them in this lifetime, the energies of your current relationship will reflect the original condition. It isn't as easy to recognize the energies as it is on the personality level because the stories aren't from this physical lifetime and your mental body has no memory of it. However, the original energies do exist in the soul levels, and can be felt as a gut feeling. Since you both feel your side of the pattern, the two of you together will create a new situation that reproduces the original condition. You may become good friends right away since there's a sense of familiarity and appreciation between you. Or, if it's a difficult relationship, you'll have a chance to resolve the story a better way this time around. The challenge is on the personality level, but the lessons are incorporated at the soul level. This is part of how we grow at the soul level.

It is also possible to have good karma. When we do kind deeds for people, or make sacrifices on their behalf, we engage with their souls in a positive way. They may return the favour at an unspecified time in the future. Negative or positive, karma is the law of consequences playing out in the soul levels. Soul level relationships happen frequently with souls we have known and liked or loved. We recognize each other at the soul level when we first meet, and feel an uncanny familiarity even though it's the first physical meeting in this lifetime. These are souls we already know well and feel comfortable with. These people often become our friends or lovers again this time around, and we continue developing deep human relationships through time.

Soul Patterns

Some karmic patterns have to do with the general outline of a persons' life. Because of choices our soul has made in previous lifetimes, we bring resulting intentions into this lifetime. These intentions can represent good consequences of things we have accomplished in the past. Our passions, talents, likes and dislikes show these general patterns of the soul field. Our soul provides the fundamental patterns for our behaviors, thoughts and responses. It gives us a certain style and disposition. We may have talent as a musician, athlete or mathematician.

The talent can reflect a history of lives lived exploring these expressions. This is certainly true of child prodigies. On a soul level, the child is already a highly gifted musician or athlete. It is just a matter of growing and training the new physical and mental bodies to pick up where he or she left off in the last lifetime.

These soul level qualities are easy to recognize when a baby is first born. Since the infant has almost no mental body yet, their personality is still almost non-existent. This makes it easier to tell what their soul is like. I have five children. I found each one to be a very unique being on the day he or she was born. I remember saying at the time of their births that they didn't have any personality yet, but they did have disposition or character. For example, my daughter was a strong, sit-up-and-take-command kind of person. She let me know exactly how she liked and didn't like being held within the first two days of her life. One of my sons I described as a deep quiet pool, observing and taking it all in for future use. These descriptions fit them as well today as on their first days.

Spiritual Contracts

Souls almost always pick familiar families to be born into. Our children and parents, siblings and spouses are usually souls we have been with in previous lifetimes. Together we work through long streams of learning over many lives. We choose to come into this lifetime in spiritual contracts together, to learn and grow. While a contract needs to exist between parents and children, a contract can exist with anyone else. It seems that we agree to act out certain energies with the other soul in this lifetime. This can reflect karmic patterning, or it can be part of the plan for the lifetime, unrelated to outstanding consequences that need to be worked out. Either is possible. Marriages, business partnerships and intense friendships often have this contractual nature. For example, my sister and I certainly agreed to be here together. We have been each other's most significant confidants throughout our lives, starting when we shared a bedroom as children. Through our adult years, we both walked our spiritual paths very deeply, sharing our teachings and resources. Now we both work as spiritual teachers and energy healers. For each of us, the spiritual work of this lifetime would have been much harder to accomplish without the other one to work it out with. Our soul level contract has been a lifelong blessing.

Other contracted patterns between people are not such happy stories. We often get dragged back into some messy relationship we left unfinished in a previous lifetime. It seems to be part of our karmic path to live through the relationship again. When we have a karmic pattern in our relationship, and we contract to work with the soul again in this lifetime, we accept a major challenge. How we align with the person this time around marks the progress of our souls. We may continue meeting in future lifetimes until we can avoid getting hooked by our own tendencies. Our learning, healing and enlightenment will change our patterns.

It is comforting to understand how the energy fields relate because we can use the knowledge to change the conditions of our lives. If there's a relationship that bothers us, we can delve into the interactions between our energy fields, our chakra expressions and our karmic experiences with the other person. If we heal our wounds that create our half of the behavior, then the relationship will transform. Because it takes two to create a pattern, when one changes, the pattern changes. You cannot be held to an old karmic pattern if you have healed your half of it, regardless of the other person's growth.

Why We Forget

There is an implication in some spiritual disciplines that we 'have to' forget our previous lives, as though we would lose some critical part of being human if we remembered. I suggest that we can live with an awareness of the existence of previous lifetimes and a sense of our soul energies, and this will in no way harm our experience as a human. Each lifetime grows a new personality, with a new mental body and a new set of beliefs and experiences. Most people have forgotten that it is possible to learn from past lives, since our culture doesn't support the idea. However, forgetting for cultural reasons does not imply that we are 'supposed to' forget. If remembering is in the divine blueprint, then it's possible to make use of remembering.

For the human soul to grow, the person has to make choices and learn from the results: trial and error, live and learn. It's important to live through the experience of the lesson. No one can learn our lessons for us, and we can't learn a lesson until we're ready for it. But when we are ready, and we go through the process, we learn. Then we incorporate the learning into our regular behavior and embody it. We usually don't remember the learning itself though. Some lessons stick with us because they were particularly painful or fun, but most slip by in our day-to-day existence. The design seems to be that we only remember aspects of the past that relate to what is going on in the present. This is true of both this lifetime and previous ones. We go up and down in small bumps as we progress upward on our journey of learning. But once we've integrated a learning, we forget what it felt like not to have accomplished that lesson. There may be little reminders, but mostly, the past is gone. Only the present exists. The same is true of lifetimes. If we have fully learned and integrated a lesson, it won't turn up again. If a lesson has turned up, we haven't learned it before, or we haven't completed our learning of it. So maybe the reason we don't remember previous lifetimes is because we don't need to. All we need to know is what our sum total self is like at any given time.

While it's the soul that progresses from lifetime to lifetime, it's the personality that actually does the learning. Situations arise and we choose how to react. Our reactions demonstrate the development of our souls and the progress we've made since the last similar challenge. When we get triggered by something and feel an emotional reaction rising up, how do we choose to respond? If a tragedy befalls us, or a crisis engulfs us, how do we respond? These are tests of the human, both personality and soul. It's not until the outer behavior is changed and the inner attitudes have evolved, that the lesson is fully integrated.

The density and intensity of the personality levels are the materials we're here to explore with. It's possible for the personality to ask for advice from the soul, and to explore soul level conditions and experiences to shed light on a current situation, but all the decision making and action depend on the personality. Ultimately, humanity is being led by its densest and most intense experiences. This is what makes us learn the way we do. The choices are up to us. So are the consequences.

The present moment is all that exists for testing and growth. We already embody everything we've learned to date. The more times we relive a lesson, the more deeply we embody it. We may need to test ourselves many times over and pass the test over and over before we're really ready to move on. The soul aspects may feel OK about the lesson, but the personality may still get triggered. No matter how advanced a soul is, if the personality still chooses to respond in a fearful and dark manner, the soul can't grow any further. The personality is a required part of the soul's growth. It is the tool for demonstrating our state of evolution and the testing ground for spiritual growth.

I remember a case in the news in which a Mennonite family lost a two-year old daughter in a highway collision between their horse-drawn buggy and a car driven by a drunk driver. The child died at the scene. Amid the pain and emotional trauma of the death of their child, the parents stayed in loving forgiveness of the driver. They accepted that their daughter's life purpose had been to help the man learn his lessons about drinking and driving. They worked with him to find help for his addiction without ever entering into shame and blame. These people faced a major test and passed through it with love and forgiveness in their hearts.

When the World Trade Towers were attacked, the collective soul of humanity underwent a massive test. Each person faced his or her own internal test from a wide set of choices on how to respond. In the immediate aftermath, while there was a voice that cried out for revenge and more violence, the collective response was gentler. The majority of people chose to respond in a more spiritually evolved manner. As a collective, the human soul responded with prayers for peace and understanding. The American group soul began to look at itself more critically than it had before. People individually responded with acts of charity and kindness. However, as the days went by, the voice of revenge grew stronger and there seemed to be less collective growth than first seemed possible. The lessons of peace, forgiveness and self-reflection were not fully integrated and will likely have to come around again.

Finally I would like to say again that the soul field is much more complex than this simple rendering can describe. Whether there are specific human souls that reincarnate exactly in new lifetimes or whether it is much more of a collective growth is not clear. However, the laws of karmic consequence, the relationships between souls and the pathways of learning at the soul level all seem to exist. What the exact processes are is still unclear. Thinking about it as individual souls with histories of lifetimes works well as a way for a person to access his or her own experience of their soul field. However, the complexity of unity consciousness begs us to stay open to much more complex organizing principles than only this individuating one.

Practical Exercises

- *Exploring the Soul Field*

To begin exploring your soul level, sit quietly and set the intention to move your point of awareness into your soul field. Allow your awareness to expand to encompass more than a foot of space around your body, and feel your awareness expanding into this area. You can move your point of awareness up and out through the crown chakra to an area about one to two feet above your head if you like. This will leave the denser dimensions of the personality below and allow you to feel the textures and themes of your soul experience better. Then feel what it is like to sit in that larger energy field. What sort of issues matter to you? How do you feel emotionally about different triggers in your life? Through observation, you may build up an awareness of when it is your personality level activating and when it is the deeper, underlying soul field that is engaging.

You may also invite yourself to feel when it is your soul field that is reacting to a person or event in your life. This may be either in a familiar and happy context or a challenging and triggering one. If it is a triggering experience, you can ask for healing or for love to be brought to your soul, and you will probably feel the reaction quieting down.

You may still want to explore your soul-level beliefs though, to see if they are spiritually true, or simply the frightened thoughts of a long-ago self. Whenever you feel an irrationally strong emotional reaction to an experience, ask yourself if the reaction is happening in your soul level. If it is, you may need to revisit a past-life experience, or at least to consider the reaction as pointing to something archetypal about humanity. You can always ask what your soul-level lesson is from the situation, and feel into the deeper aspects of self that show up. The issues usually feel more archetypal, more persistent and less rational. They may not make sense in your current life, yet still seem to plague you. Engaging with your higher energies to bring a more spiritually true perspective into the original story will always bring a sense of peace and completion. This is how the soul field is healed.

Over time you will develop an awareness of what your soul feels like compared to your personality. You may recognize the talents and passions that have underlain your entire life as part of your soul's expression. Sometimes you may feel a strong desire to pursue something new, like traveling to a new place or learning to play a musical instrument. As you progress along this path of learning, you may feel as though it is your soul that is developing. Overall, the more you can bring awareness to the contribution of your soul field to your daily existence, the richer your experience will become.

Chapter Six

The Higher Dimensions

Beyond the soul level come higher dimensions of spirit that have no physical or etheric form. Between the soul and the eighteenth chakra we seem to be part of vast streams of conscious energy where we know ourselves as spirit only. In these dimensions the experience still has a sense of a separable spiritual self while also feeling relationships with other spirit beings. There continues to be a sense of self and relationship, a personal aspect and a community aspect, an introverted self and an extroverted self. Beyond the eighteenth chakra however, it seems there is only the One Self, the Godself. In the unified dimension beyond the eighteenth there is no separation possible. Everything is part of the One Self.

As we begin to explore the spiritual realms, we face the cultural problem of exploring in isolated groups. In these realms there's little human experience and even less group awareness. Separated individuals and communities develop different practices and language. While this establishes possibilities within the human soul fabric that anyone can access, we still find ourselves working independently of each other. There's no collective understanding to describe our experiences of the higher energies. Each group ends up creating language of its own to describe experiences and to refer to spiritual locations. We may all be experiencing the same dimension, or we may be all over the nonphysical map! How are we to know and begin to cross-fertilize our understandings? I decided that mapping out the higher chakras one-by-one and relating them to our human experiences was a good starting point for finding common ground and creating common language. In this context I share my language and understanding. I know it is only a sketch or a working model, but I offer it as a place to start in developing collective awareness about our spiritual nature. It's also straightforward and simple so anyone can use it to explore on his or her own.

My understanding of these higher chakras has come from years of dedicated exploration both in my own energy field and with clients and students individually and in groups. The model I share with you has been developed through combining the information provided in the esoteric writings of Alice Bailey and others with these thousands of individual explorations. The interesting thing about this model is that it isn't mysterious or magical. It's simple and straightforward. It collects together a lot of disparate bits and gives them a cohesive whole. When people work with this outline and move through meditation to access the spiritual realms of the higher dimensions, they always get there. Naturally their experiences are unique, but there are recognizable similarities among us all. It's the similarities I've developed into the understanding of the higher dimensions that I present to you here. I'll give a brief overview of each dimension and then a more detailed look at each.

The language I use to describe the higher dimensions starts from the esoteric literature of Alice Bailey, Djwhal Khul and others in the same tradition. Their writings refer to the higher chakras but without giving information about them. They also name them with strange words such as Atmic and Logoic. I choose instead to give the chakras and dimensions names that relate to the experience of being there. The exception is the Monad which is a word so well used in the esoteric works that it already has a foundation on which to build. The Monadic dimension is found between chakras ten and twelve. It is the pure spiritual nature of the human experience. Expanding to the Monad at the twelfth chakra and integrating the spiritual understandings into daily life is all an individual needs to live a deeply satisfying, peaceful life of love and creativity.

Beyond the Monad, in chakras thirteen to fifteen, is what I think of as the Master level. It is the dimension through which direct orders are received from beyond and carried out. It is the level to access for communication with Ascended Master energies and where the Masters can be found for teachings. It is also where an individual's personal mastery is accessed. When an individual begins channeling Master level energies into his or her life, there is no stopping the work. The individual can't not do it. There is a powerful compulsion to do the work as directed. At the Master level the individual becomes an active agent in the unfolding of the universe.

Beyond the Master level, in chakras sixteen to eighteen, is what I refer to as the Co-Creative level, or what a client-friend calls 'All-That-Is'. It is where energy streams first separate out from the unified source field into identifiably unique aspects. These are energies of a magnitude so vast that the limited human mind can't comprehend them at all. This is where the Rays emanate from, and where streams like Christ Consciousness emerge from our One whole Godself. This is also where dark energy is first created as a stream without love. The co-creative level is where the creative process of expressing life in all its physical and nonphysical forms begins.

The universe as we know it emerges at the co-creative level, as do universes of other types. There are universes made up of light and sound and other forms that are completely unlike our physical universe. Each one is conscious, but the styles of consciousness differ. There are some overlaps between human life and consciousness from these other realms, such as the colored light-shapes of the Language of Light[15], and other forms of non-conceptual consciousness. Translating from these other worlds back to our own is tricky since the form of consciousness is fundamentally different. For people who feel inspired to explore in very 'other-worldly' places, meditating straight up through the crown to the seventeenth chakra and then heading out in any direction will yield very 'far-out' experiences. It's always important to go straight up through the crown and not to angle out from the top of the forehead. The top part of the third eye chakra, what you could think of as the crown of the third eye, is a very imaginative place, but is not the same as the spiritual realms themselves. To access the realms, one needs to move straight up through the crown, leaving the denser dimensions below.

Beyond the eighteenth chakra is our One self, our Godself, our Source, or the Absolute. Exploring beyond the eighteenth leaves little one can say or write. The experience is unspeakable. While our human consciousness is equipped to process aspects of the experiences, our human culture has no words or concepts to attach to the experiences. The sense is of only one self, with all the atoms of the universe as a body and all the streams of consciousness as expressions of self. The absolute energy is one of absolute love, huge golden fire, and unspeakable presence and power.

Let us now explore each of these higher dimensions in more detail.

The Monad

The monad is the first spiritual dimension beyond the human soul level. It's easy to access, and contains the aspects of self we commonly think of as the Higher Self, Over-Soul, IAM Presence or Super-Ego. In it we find the unconditionally loving nature of spirit. The monad oversees and supports the soul and physical creations in the denser dimensions. The Higher Self is completely and unconditionally accepting, non-judging and compassionate in its help. It is peaceful, wise and insightful. Being able to access the monadic energies at will changes the entire nature of human experience. Living from the monad is truly living 'the Kingdom of God on earth'.

The Monadic dimension is found between the tenth and twelfth chakras. It is considerably larger than the soul field, measuring roughly ten to fifteen feet across. It surrounds and inter-penetrates both the soul and personality dimensions. It is pure spirit energy, without any physical form at all. Figure 6 gives an artistic impression of what the monadic field looks like, although the field is actually more rounded and less pointy. All energy that takes etheric or physical form in the soul or personality levels has been stepped down by the monad. The monad enables souls to exist, just as the soul enables the physical body to exist. All formed life seems to be stepped down through a monad into the soul level and then into physicality. Like a system of locks that control the flow of water, the monad, soul and personality bring vast spirit energies into more defined and manageable units. If all life-forms have a monadic dimension, then any other life-form can be contacted through the eleventh chakra in the monadic dimension. Just as all humanity is connected through the human soul, so all formed life may be connected through the monad.

The tenth chakra anchors all the much higher energies into the Monad. It also makes the monadic and higher levels available to the soul. When the soul wants to incorporate spiritual energies into its human experience, the person can open to the monadic dimension through the tenth chakra. The soul and personality meet their own spiritual energy and can be guided by the wisdom and unconditional acceptance of the higher self. In the Monadic field, spiritual guidance is readily available. There is a feeling of being part of a loving community, observing and helping in the unfolding of human experience. The eleventh chakra is the relationship chakra of the Monadic self. Angels, spirit guides and other unseen beings are engaged with there. People who channel off-planet intelligences also seem to be connecting through the eleventh chakra.

Figure 6 - The Monadic Field or the Higher Self

The Monad

The twelfth chakra is the individuated monadic self. It is the Higher Self, the wise, eternal, beyond-human spirit self that guides all human activities at the soul and personality levels. Expanding to the Monadic level energies feels like 'coming home'. It is where we first experience the essential feeling of the great oneness of all being. We are purely spirit, with no strings attached. The energies are vast, hugely expansive and deeply loving. They are infinite and instantaneous, full and empty. There is a sense of pure light, often white, although the light may also have colors present. There is a knowingness of being one with all life on a spiritual level. There is a sense of peace and happiness, of joy and comfort.

At the monadic level, there is no attachment to the personal life, although we still love it and enjoy it. Every aspect of life is motivated by love and service. The only response to suffering of any kind is deep compassion. The way humans create their reality through illusion is clearly seen and understood. An individual living from the monadic level is able to take full responsibility for his or her own reality and live from their deepest truth. They are also able to see the projection of another person's illusion and not get caught in it. Intuition becomes reality. The experience of life comes to be felt and known rather than thought. Nonphysical life gets taken for granted. We merge with the web of life and know we can rely on it to meet all our needs. We feel like spirit having a human experience.

Christ Consciousness speaks directly to us at the monadic level. We can be guided and taught daily by Masters, Archangels and other spiritual teachers from the higher realms. We have a deep sense of joy and thanksgiving, experiencing the bigger picture and feeling our place in its unfolding. We know we are in the world, yet not limited to being of it only. There is a great sense of compassion for the working human self, with all our traumas and troubles. Yet, the problems of daily life seem to dissolve away. There is always a simple and loving solution available. The human self can always ask for help and receive an abundance of spiritual teaching and assistance. We see all other humans with a deep sense of compassion for their struggles. Abiding love is unquestioned.

The Master Level

The next dimension, between chakras thirteen and fifteen, is entirely different from all the levels leading up to and including the Monad. I call it the Master level. I have no idea what it may have been called by others as I've never read anything that talks about it explicitly. This dimension is limitless and infinite. It has no edges and feels unbounded. The energies are hugely powerful and unstoppable. There is an all-encompassing power of spiritual intention and absolute purpose of God-inspired passion. Gone is the serene watcher of the Monad. Gone too is the calm feeling of being in our spiritual home. These are replaced with the absolute power of God's will.

At the Master level the human form is recognized as a co-creative agent that exists to carry out higher-order spiritual intentions. The human self doesn't feel separated from God in any way or in any dimension. There is recognition and compassion for the physical body and the human experience that serves as the vehicle for the work, although there is little direct input regarding human experience. The Master level is not where you go for advice on your personal growth and spiritual enlightenment. It is where you go to receive orders for your work on the planet. There is a huge amount of spiritual guidance at this level for connecting directly with God Consciousness in order to be a more fully surrendered agent of God's work. If there is a divine plan, the work of creating it is probably being carried out from the thirteenth to the fifteenth chakra levels.

The Master level energies anchor into the field at the thirteenth chakra. The fourteenth is where you can communicate with Master teachers such as Jesus, Mary, Buddha, Djwhal Khul, Kuthumi, Melchisadek, St. Germaine, and hundreds of other named and unnamed Beings. This is where you can find the Ashrams of the Masters that house the great spiritual energies that work to guide spiritual life on Earth. It is possible to visit with these Teachers by meditating up and out the crown chakra. You will likely be met and taken to an etheric Ashram for initiation and teaching. Often these experiences take place at night in what feel like altered dream states. Over time, you will feel the continual Presence of the Master with whom you work, almost as though you are becoming part of that Master's body in this plane of existence. Your personal work will dovetail with the work of that Master on the Earth.

A person doesn't normally engage with Master level energies unless they are compelled to be in service to the big work of Spirit on the planet. The desire or need to contact these energies may reflect a pre-birth contract to perform such spiritual duties. For most people, living with access to the monadic field is all they ever require. However, sometimes a person feels called to Master level work and intends to connect but isn't able to. In these cases it seems the Master level is not yet ready to be accessed and upward meditations will stop in the Monadic level. If you feel called to Master level work and choose to access the Master dimension through your crown chakra, you may reach what feels like a ceiling beyond your Monadic field. If this is the case, be patient; learn your spiritual lessons of compassion, integrity and whatever else you are shown, and work diligently to clear your dark areas in the lower fields. The Master level energies are too powerful to bring through a crimped field. Alice Bailey refers to such a ceiling as a 'ring-pass-not', as in a ring that you can't pass through yet. If you are pure in your intentions, know that you will begin to pass through into the next stage when your higher energies have signaled that you are prepared for it.

As we begin to engage with Master level energies, we come onstream in our own Mastery through the fifteenth chakra. Over the course of time, probably over many lifetimes, we become able to carry the Masterful energies in our human state. As we incorporate more of the teachings and hone our ability to carry these energies in our actual lives, our spiritual work on the planet becomes more and more central to our existence. Ultimately, the Master level work can't not be done; we find ourselves as servants of God Consciousness in human form without question, resistance or reservation. There is no fear. We will do whatever is required to further our work of Spirit on the planet, without consideration for how it affects our human existence. In all respects, our human existence is known to be only a vehicle for the work of Spirit.

Master level work is often of a direct spiritual nature, such as spiritual teaching or healing. However, being an open conduit for spirit work from this level can also take form in the arts. Great painters, composers or musicians have also been channeling the work of the Master dimension to the human community. The compulsion of work that can't not be done is recognized in these artistic geniuses. This overarching need to do this spiritual work is a normal feature of Master level experience.

The Co-Creative Dimension

My own experience with the energies of the next dimension is limited. I have visited many times, but each visit is totally unique. I may be entirely wrong in thinking there is only one dimension before unity consciousness at the eighteenth chakra. Or it could be that I'm roughly correct in thinking that all the other dimensions that can be accessed from there branch out from the seventeenth chakra. I can't tell. What I can say so far is that the energies in the sixteenth to eighteenth chakras are unimaginably vast and powerful. At the eighteenth, it seems the Rays of consciousness emerge from the unified field to enable the unfolding of expressed life in all its forms, both physical and nonphysical. At this level there's a knowing of the vast movements in linear time including a deep knowing of the growth path of humanity over tens of thousands of years and of conscious life over billions of Earth years. There is also a knowing of the non-linearity of time, of its flow and patterning as one of our Godself's creative instruments. Time is felt as both instantaneous and infinite. Simultaneity of all life is known. Manifestation from the web of life comes almost immediately.

This dimension is so vast that the experiences of it are indescribable in human terms. However, there is still a sense of a separable self as well as relations with other streams of energy. The self of the eighteenth chakra still has a familiar ring to it, a template of Self that is recognizable albeit very unlike the self of the lower dimensions. There are also other energies to communicate with at the seventeenth chakra although they may feel like an entire universe. They branch out at right angles from this universal stream we inhabit. These other dimensions are so unlike this one that they require a bending of human consciousness to be able to explore them at all. For me, bringing back any usable 'information' from such explorations seems almost impossible, although knowing they exist is fascinating. I expect that much of the leading edge of new consciousness is appearing through people who have visited the alternate realms that can be accessed here. I think of 'The Book of Knowledge: The Keys of Enoch' by J. J. Hurtak as a good example.[16]

It seems there are still teachers and guiding energies in the co-creative dimension. These energies teach the Masters. It seems that part of the work of this dimension is to embody more God consciousness in whatever form the being is in, be it physical, etheric or spirit. The manipulating of physical laws is taught here. Knowing the self as one aspect-stream of God enables the movement back and forth between Godself consciousness and the potential for creation of anything. It is this potential that makes me call this the 'co-creative' level. In the unified field of our Godself, everything is possible. All we need is to decide to will it into existence through the power of love. The rare human sage who integrates the energies of this field in his or her form can perform the miracles of manifestation, bi-location and eternal life.

Unified Consciousness

Beyond the eighteenth chakra is the experience of our Godself where we are God Consciousness, the Unified Self, the real IAM Presence, only One Being. All life everywhere shows the face of God, and only the face of God. There is no other experience. There is no possibility of a separated self. We are One Being. The plants, animals and star systems are felt extensions of our body and experienced as Self. Every human is an aspect of our one body. All conscious life in every dimension is a felt expression of the Self. Everything lives in a communal consciousness of radiant love. Separated streams of existence are felt as streams in the ocean, separate, yet part of the unified whole. Individuated consciousness can move freely between any of the forms. All the denser dimensions are experienced in their purity. Darkness exists only as a building block of the creation of experience. Everything is lived as an aspect of radiant conscious love. We swim in the ocean of divine bliss.

Beyond the eighteenth chakra there are no individuated streams of consciousness. Moving through the eighteenth, everything dissolves back into the unified whole. There is no separated self at all. Physical bodies are experienced as light patterns resonating and vibrating with the holy Love of God. Each body is experienced taking its correct place within the entirety of creation. Every living thing is made of the radiant presence of conscious love and is experienced that way from within the human perspective. Communication with all formed life including angels, plants or air molecules is simultaneous and instantaneous, because there is only One self, experiencing through our many creative forms. The Oneness of self includes all differentiated aspects, in every dimension. The individuated aspect is the experience of being a living sun, radiant, holy and vast beyond human comprehension. The collective aspect is The Absolute.

Living this expanded experience is becoming a cell of God's body. Mind becomes God's consciousness. Will becomes God's intention. Love becomes God's essence. 'I' becomes an expression of God. Anything that was ever recognized as a separated self dissolves entirely. There is no separated I, there is only We as a collective of One Self, rather like the 'royal we'. The experience is one of such intense rapture that the physical form can barely stand the power of it. It is the bliss sought after by mystics through the ages. And it's available to everyone beyond the eighteenth chakra.

Since spiritual growth comes in states and stages, it's possible to attain states of awareness during meditations and dream states in which these very high dimensions are accessible. Information and teachings can be downloaded in these episodes, to be made use of during subsequent human experiences. However, walking the daily life of a human being from the expanded states is a different matter. Knowing all life as your body, and all humans as yourself is so far outside 'normal' experience there are no words or collective culture to house it. It creates a weird reality to live in the world of illusion with humans who believe the illusion, while seeing so far beyond it all. Traditionally, gurus have lived in isolated communities where people have sought them out for teachings, cared for their bodily needs and received energetic templates directly by being close to the master. However, in this new age of Aquarian awareness, it seems that the whole point is to integrate these vast understandings and experiences into the regular human world. Hence there are teachers who are living from the higher dimensions scattered throughout our communities, working to bring in the new enlightened human world.

Practical Exercises

- *Exploring the Higher Dimensions*

To access any of the higher dimensions, bring your awareness deep inside your head and fully into the central channel. Next begin to move your point of conscious awareness straight up and away from your body in a slow progression. Notice the movements from chakra to chakra and rest in each new dimension until it feels like time to move higher. You may spend weeks or months investigating the experience of a new level of your field. It may happen that you feel as though you're running up against a ceiling that can't be passed through. If so, over the course of time these ceilings will soften and eventually the center will begin to open. The existence of a ceiling indicates either that there is a block or that your guiding self senses your human self isn't quite ready to experience the energies from beyond. It can be that the energies from the lower dimensions haven't been integrated enough yet and progression to the higher energies is being stopped from the spiritual side. This is a protection of the human self by the higher self. You may also run into blockages of dark energy that prevent you from moving up and out. These blocks can contain congestion from old experiences in this lifetime or earlier ones. Blocks of this type can be cleared with the regular techniques of energy healing.

Remember that each dimension is nested within the larger ones, so in fact, they are all present within your body. Ultimately you can know how each dimension feels within your human form. A wonderful way to explore and integrate the higher dimensions is to move out through the crown to access them, but once firmly established in a field, then bring your awareness back down to how your body, emotions and mind feel while experiencing that higher dimension of self. Places in the denser fields that can't resonate with the higher energies will make themselves known to you. Over the course of time, as you process whatever arises for you from these experiences, your denser fields will become lighter and better able to vibrate with the higher energies. Eventually you may come to recognize the experiences of the different dimensions and you will be able to meditate directly into them without going up and out through the crown chakra. Then you will be able to access the higher levels of consciousness at will.

A good meditation to develop the ability to feel the different dimensions within the body is one that moves your awareness deeper and deeper into the physical body. You move your conscious awareness inside and then keep moving deeper behind whatever you find. As you continue to 'go behind' while staying within the body, you will continue to move into more expanded dimensions of your energy field. Ultimately you can experience the unified Godself right in the core of your physical body. Because the Heart is the chakra that anchors all the higher energies of love into the human dimension, the easiest and most wonderful way to experience the power and ecstacy of God consciousness within the body is through the deepest dimensions of the Heart.

So far in this book, I have provided information about the different energy fields and how to access them. Now we address questions regarding living from the subtle fields. How does life change as a person integrates consciousness from the higher dimensions into everyday life? The remaining chapters examine different aspects of living from the whole you.

Chapter Seven

Making Use of Guidance

Having worked our way through an exploration of all the energy fields, we can now begin to make use of the information. In this chapter we examine how we can enhance our day to day lives by accessing guidance and insight from our spiritual dimensions. To live in open communication with our spiritual energies is a natural skill, like talking. But like talking, it requires a process of learning. We can learn to ask questions and to interpret the answers that come from our own higher dimensions with some degree of accuracy. We can also learn to stay aware of on-going subtle experiences so our spiritual consciousness can access our human state at any time. Living in this open flow of communication allows our working human selves to be supported, guided, challenged and inspired by our spiritual base.

Remember we are each a collective of energies that co-exist in different dimensions. We have at least a human, soul, monadic, master, pure conscious and unified Godself. Our human self is capable of interacting with and receiving guidance from any of the other levels. It's probably true that any part can communicate with any other part, and maybe they do, but since we're so embedded in our human aspects, we may only be aware of communications that involve our personality or soul levels. We also have friends and teachers in each dimension, just as we have friends in our physical life, and we can receive communication from them too. Any time we need help with a question or some good advice, we can always ask. Whenever we ask, we will be answered. And, if we're open at all times, we will also receive input when we're not expecting it. This open flow of ready exchange in our stream of consciousness enables us as Spirit to fully embrace and inhabit our human lives. The desire for communication is a two-way street.

The first step in dialoguing with spirit is to receive the input. The second step is to interpret it. The two different steps require different skills. But people hoping for spiritual guidance are often impatient and unwittingly combine the two steps into one. As soon as they sense they might be getting a message, they immediately jump to 'what does it mean?' This throws them into their third eye mental bodies where they are no longer receptive. To receive incoming messages, we have to be connected to our subtle fields and aware of subtle sensations. When we're out in front of our foreheads, lost in our thoughts, we can't feel what's happening in the rest of our energy fields. To receive energetic input, it helps if the energy fields are quiet and calm. The art of receiving includes the ability to be patient.

If a person is fully engaged in the mental body of his third eye and busy with a stream of thoughts, his consciousness will not be ready to notice spiritual input. There must be some space available to pay attention to incoming information. To receive from spirit, the trick is to allow consciousness to flow without using all of it in thinking. It is like bi-locating consciousness so some is thinking and paying attention to the personality world while other parts are paying attention to the subtle realms. Part of the stream of consciousness remains quiet and still, in a witnessing state. Like listening in the physical dimension, if a person thinks and talks non-stop, everything that happens in his world is generated from within his own mind. But if he can also quietly listen, he no longer controls everything in his domain and can become receptive to new information. So it is with receiving from spirit. The person needs to witness his or her stream of consciousness, allowing part of it to feel idle and receptive in order to notice when unexpected information comes in. With practice, a person can think and do all the activities of daily life while remaining open to spiritual input.

Consider an example of the normal way people miss out on spiritual advice by jumping to their minds too quickly. Suppose a person has been working with a guiding energy she relates to as a guardian angel and the on-going message has been to lighten her load. Then one day she receives a message that appears as a vision of an old suitcase. If she does the usual thing, she will leap to her familiar third eye patterns and think "That's my angel telling me to lighten my load again. It's a heavy suitcase, like my burden." This is a classic example of the mental body of the third eye interpreting the input too quickly. The ideas are familiar and they come immediately. But if she sat quietly in stillness while the vision was appearing, or re-visited the moment after it had occurred, she might have noticed that it felt different from the inputs that came from the angel. Maybe the angel arrives with a shaft of light from above, whereas this vision came with a feeling of warmth in her back. It's a different spirit energy communicating with her. If she allowed the message of the suitcase to come in fully without trying to interpret too quickly, she might have sensed it suggesting that "It would be good to move from this apartment." By being too hasty and by wanting to know the meaning too quickly, she would have lost the opportunity for an important piece of guidance.

Learning to hone intuition and spiritual guidance is like learning to play a musical instrument. At first you can't do much. You start by practicing scales and playing simple pieces. As you practice though, your skill develops and you learn to play more complicated things. Eventually, if you keep up with the practicing and playing, you master your instrument. If you stop using the instrument, your skill declines. In the physical world, the music can be heard by other people who provide feedback. However, with spiritual practice, all the feedback is internal. It's like being your own audience. If you use your spiritual channel in service to other people, you may receive feedback if they say the message was meaningful. This outer feedback is helpful, but it is a bonus. In general, you have to be able to tell from inside whether your interpretation is accurate or not. It's like a musician practicing without an audience who has to develop an inner ear to tell how he sounds. The spiritual seeker has to develop inner signals to tell whether he is accurate or not in his reception and interpretation. This means that the wounded ego and its dark voices can have a field day with spiritual work if they are not kept under a watchful eye. Honing the subtle fields as receptors, and developing critical interpretive skills that avoid using the normal mind will help keep the ego in check.

Spirit communicates with the personality in many different ways. For example, communications can come in through the spiritual dimensions of the third eye chakra including signs, symbols and visions. These inputs are decidedly different from normal thoughts and need to be interpreted carefully. Spirit can also communicate its presence through any other chakra, especially the heart and solar plexus. Here the input is more likely a sensation, like a pressure, or warmth or a wavy feeling, or it may be nothing more than a sense of knowing something is happening. The inputs are very subtle. The more still and quiet a person's field is, the more likely he or she is to notice the signals.

Receiving Input

In order to recognize spiritual input, you first need to know what your own mental input feels like so you can tell the difference. You can tell when you are having thoughts by sensing where in your energy field your point of awareness is located. If it is out in front of your forehead, or out the sides of your head above your ears, you are operating from your thinking self, in the mental body of the third eye chakra. If your eyes are darting around, this is a good indicator that your awareness is in the third eye mental body of the personality level. When your mental body is active, thoughts come very quickly, tumbling on each other, and you often repeat the same thought over and over. You often hear your thoughts in words spoken inside your head. In the functioning of the brain, thoughts relate to the electrical charges flowing along dendrites. Electricity is of the fire element so thoughts are quick. There is no lull between having a thought and knowing what the thought is. It is immediate. Thoughts are also intense. They command your attention. It is easy to be swept along by them. You can also recognize your thoughts as ideas you've had before. Or, if it is a new thought, it develops in a logical way out of thoughts you are accustomed to. Some people are more creative thinkers, creating more new thoughts, and others are more traditional thinkers, preferring familiar thoughts. But either way, thoughts are familiar or logically related.

Receiving input from spirit dimensions doesn't feel at all like thinking. Usually incoming signals from spirit move more slowly, like a breeze passing through. There is often a subtle indicator that something is happening or about to happen, but with no content yet. Sometimes the message comes instantaneously through direct knowing, but is located deep within the body or head and not out in front of the forehead. It is usually surprising, and doesn't follow from any previous thoughts. Sometimes there is a sense of a presence, or of another Being somewhere close by. Sometimes the message comes in words, but the words don't originate in front of the forehead. Sometimes the words appear in letters being spelled out. One client saw them being written across the ceiling. Another saw them in large block letters across her whole internal field of vision.

When spirit communicates through visions, the picture is received deep in the interior of the head, like a nighttime dream, not in front of the forehead like an imagination. Most people do not receive much visual stimulus, even though modern spiritual styles often expect people to use visualizations. I suspect this desire to 'see' follows from living in a culture that is so oriented to how things look. With photography, movies, mirrors and attention to looks, our spiritual exercise has gotten skewed away from our more natural condition of sensing. People often get frustrated, thinking spirit isn't communicating with them, when in fact they are receiving a lot of information but it is not visual. Other times it is clear that people are making stuff up in their minds while believing spirit is communicating with them through visualizations. In fact, most people are more clairsentient than clairvoyant, getting their information through sensing with their whole energy field rather than only through the third eye. Teachers sometimes press their students to develop visual skills. This can easily lead the student mistakenly to creating a picture with the mind and thinking it is a vision coming from spirit.

For most people, perceiving energy works best by opening the whole field to incoming messages and letting the visual component take a back seat. Those people to whom spirit naturally appears in visuals will know and can work from there. Having worked with thousands of people, my estimate is that only about 10 to 20 percent are naturally inclined to visual input. The rest work much better through sensing the energies directly. Some people hear the energies or smell them too. Remember, there is no spiritual hierarchy that says one form of experience is better than another. Whatever works for you is right for you. There can be excessive ego attached to 'seeing' spirit visually and spiritual status accorded to people who see or claim to see. This is a good example of the personality creating a spiritual hierarchy that doesn't actually exist.

In whatever way spirit communicates though, it can be recognized as spirit because it does not feel like 'self'. The more a person is aware of his or her own personal patterns of thoughts and emotions, the more that person will be able to recognize when something else is happening. The best advice for receiving from spirit includes knowing your own inner habits. Observe your own patterns of thoughts and interpretations. Become aware of how you respond emotionally to various topics. The more you know your own responses, the more easily you can perceive through them. If you can recognize what is your own contribution, you will be more able to recognize what is not.

Let's focus now on how to receive incoming signals. First, you need to be still and quiet and to disconnect from your mental body. It works best if you pull your point of awareness in behind your forehead and drop slowly down into your heart chakra, or expand up and out through the crown chakra, as in the exercises in earlier chapters. You also need to connect with the energies of your higher self and your spirit guidance. You can do this purely with intention. Sit quietly and still your mind. Now call in your Higher Self and your Guides, and wait. The words you use don't really matter. You can try out different terms until you find the ones that resonate best in your field. Some people call in their Higher Self, or their Sacred Self, Holy Self, Spiritual Self, Original Self, I AM Presence or God Self. Some people name certain spiritual energies, such as the Angels or the Archangels, Divine Mother, Christ Consciousness, St. Germaine, Baba Gi, Jesus, Mary or Buddha. Some people have personal guides they know by name, such as Jessie, or Big Bear. Some people imagine sitting in a field of white light with the vibration of Love passing through. Some people imagine a beautiful scene from a favorite place to feel the peace and deep love that can open in nature. Some people chant or sing or move in a special way that opens them to their depths. It doesn't matter how you connect with your higher energies as long as you end up feeling their presence.

You will feel slight changes in your field and in your body as the different energies merge with you. You might relax, or sigh deeply. You might feel a particular sensation as a spirit energy makes itself known to you. With practice, you will come to recognize these subtle signals. It is good to listen and perceive with your whole energy field. It is important to stay away from your third eye mental body while this process is occurring. Otherwise you may start actively thinking, and miss the opportunity to receive from spirit. The skill is to learn to stay receptive and aware and capable of interpreting while not ending up in the familiar mind. I think of this as using the higher mind. It is possible to develop consciousness and awareness in the third eye in the higher dimensions without getting stuck in the personality level.

Now you can make use of the connection you have set up. It is helpful to make a statement of intention at first, to establish throughout your field what your focus is. For example, you might say you intend to develop your ability to communicate with spirit energies, or to seek guidance on a certain topic. After you become more skilled at dialoguing you probably won't need to do this, but it always helps to focus intention. As you explore and experience, you will build up a community of spirit energies that help you. Each one will have a different energetic template and will be helpful to you for different purposes. As you progress through the years, the guides who work with you will evolve along with you, although some people walk a lifetime in which it is appropriate to stay with one guiding group and go deeper and deeper into one realm. There are no rules about what is right or wrong. Everyone is unique. What matters is to create your own sacred alchemy that feels right for you. If you let Spirit guide you, you will find what works best for you.

Asking Questions

Communicating with Spirit is a skill. The best way to develop any skill is to start with simple tasks. The simplest task of communicating is to ask questions. Later on you will recognize spiritual input whether you have asked a question or not, but to start, you need to know what you're waiting for. The first step is to ask for a yes signal and a no signal. Close your eyes, sit quietly, connect with your higher energies and slowly ask for a yes signal. Pay attention to all subtle indicators. Repeat the process until you are sure of the signal. When you have a good sense of your yes signal, repeat the process asking for a no signal.

Your signals might be a pressure, warmth, sensation, tightening, a wavy feeling or an expansion. They might be a picture, color or sound. They could be anything. Examples from students include a pressure in the lower back, feeling touched on the cheek, a red swirl going from right to left and blue from left to right, a tightening in the neck, heat in the hands, an opening in the chest and a skull and crossbones appearing in the inner vision. You can ask repeatedly until you are sure of your signal. Hone your receptivity by sitting in stillness and recognizing what is incoming. The signals you receive will stay with you forever. Once you have established them, they don't change. You can then use these signals to answer simple yes/no questions. Test it out a bit until you trust yourself in it. If your mind is getting involved, you may not be able to tell whether it's accurate or not. This is the time to go deep within your head, far behind the workings of your mental body and brain, and either move up and out the crown or drop deeply into the heart. Only by leaving the mind can we figure out what is spirit and what is our own mental offering.

When working with more complicated questions, you need to hone the question to a simple statement. Spirit can't answer complex questions. The wording needs to be specific. Suppose you feel drawn to change your occupation, but you don't know what you want to do. Your big question is "What should I do with my life?" But this is not a question anyone else can answer for you, not even your higher self. Only you can discover what you should do with your life. So you need to hone the question to a simpler one. You might ask "What is my next step?" or "What am I overlooking?" Or you might have a specific thing you're considering, such as becoming a gardener, and you can ask if that's a good idea or not. You could ask "Is it right for me to go into gardening?" Using your yes/no signals, you can elicit some answers and direction.

To ask a more complicated question, such as "what is my next step?" begin by sitting quietly and connecting. Then let your question rise up from within you, as a felt sensation, with or without words. This feeling in your body is the thing you want help with rather than the worded form of it in your third eye. Now ask the question deep in your heart or out your crown chakra, and sit in quiet stillness and wait. After a few moments you will feel a pattern of energy making its way into your body. It may come quickly or slowly, from above or behind. It may seem to appear suddenly from nowhere, or it may have a distinct route it follows into your field. There may be heat or cold, pressure or wind. You may hear words or smell scents. You may see visions or symbols, or it may come as immediate, direct knowing. Any and all methods for spirit to access you are available. Anything can happen. It is important to explore all possible avenues to know what the possibilities are, and what your area of strength is.

The only thing that can happen that would <u>not</u> be an incoming message from spirit is activity in your mental body out around your forehead. That will be your own mind, pretending to be spirit. You will feel yourself thinking familiar thoughts and recognize your eager-beaver self, like teacher's pet, wanting to know the answer too quickly. Or you might hear the cranky voices of dark consciousness in your head offering depressing or mean answers. Relax again, come inside behind the forehead again, and drop slowly down into your heart or move up through your crown again. Now put out your question again. Have no pre-conceptions. Wait for something unexpected. If you can't predict it, you can't control it. Let yourself be surprised.

Interpreting Accurately

Once the input has appeared in your field and you have received it, now comes the challenge of interpreting it accurately. If you immediately bounce out to your mental body with the input, you'll get it wrong. It is important to stay in the quiet inner stream of consciousness and work from there. Your inner wisdom comes from overlapping your heart with your third eye. You receive the information in your core, but you need to use the mind to turn it into words and concepts. The difficulty is in getting the right words and concepts. One way to do this is by comparing energetic templates.

A template is a pattern of energy vibrations. It is the energetic blueprint of the consciousness it represents. It can be simple or complex. It can be in one dimension or multi-dimensional. It is the pattern of the consciousness itself. You could imagine it like a matrix diagram, a computer graphics sequence, a complex musical sound or a mathematical formula. Homeopathic remedies are examples of energetic templates. Every word in a language has an energetic template. The word represents a pattern of consciousness. There is much more conscious reality encoded in a word that just the conceptual meaning. The concept can be described with other words, as we find in a dictionary. But the template can only be experienced directly, as a feeling. The feeling is a combination of the collective meaning of the word plus your own personal use of it. It is useful to relate to language as a series of templates.

Sometimes you find yourself in a conversation with someone who uses words differently than you do. Then you can pick up on the template of the meaning they have, and find a word in your language use that feels the same way. I think most of us do this without realizing that's what we're doing.

Every incoming message from spirit has an energetic template since it is a pattern of consciousness. Therefore, you can work to find the words that most closely match the energetic frequency of the message you received. You begin by bringing the template of the message from your heart up to the bottom of your third eye and begin scanning for a match. You can imagine it like radar. You are scanning for any words or concepts you know that come close to matching the energy template of the message. Certain words will jump up and you can piece them together. In this way you will receive an accurate message.

Here's an example of what happened once in a workshop where I was teaching this material. A man and woman who didn't know each other were working together as partners. The exercise was to receive an answer from spirit for your partner's question. The woman asked "What should I do to help my writing?" The man received a signal, feeling it deep in his body, but he immediately jumped to his mind with it. He replied "practice". I pointed out that he had created the interpretation in the mental body of his third eye and asked him to try again. He did so, and as he allowed the energy to reveal itself to him by scanning for an energetic match, he pieced together the message "write what you know". This made no sense to him. 'Practice' made sense. His mind believed that to become a better writer, the woman should practice. But he had no way of understanding the message to 'write what she knew'. However, the woman understood immediately. She wrote children's books, and Spirit was guiding her to write about what she was familiar with. She had young children. The message was to observe her own life closely, and to write from her own experience. This was a very useful piece of advice for her and not one she had thought of on her own. The man was astonished it had worked. By scanning for matching energies, he had interpreted accurately for her.

Another way of accessing a message directly is to move your point of awareness into the message itself. Suppose a bird hops onto your windowsill and you get the feeling that spirit is trying to communicate with you. Close your eyes, pull your point of awareness inside and connect with your higher energies. Then keep moving your point of awareness down through your body, down below your body into the floor, through the floor, up the wall into the windowsill and finally into the bird. As you meet the consciousness in the bird, the message from spirit will transfer immediately into your field. You're likely to get it through direct knowing at that point, although you may still need to sit with it to allow the full interpretation to become clear. Make sure you aren't sitting there with your point of awareness locked in your third eye and pretending a visualization of going to meet the bird. Instead, live through the actual experience of moving your point of awareness geographically until you meet the bird. Using the third eye to imagine it feels like having an idea while actually doing it feels like having a real experience. They feel entirely different.

There are a few simple rules for interpreting spirit guidance that will help you know if you have it right or not. First, a genuine communication from spirit feels like an experience rather than a thought. You can feel that something subtle is happening that goes beyond the mental activity of your mind. The more familiar you are with what your own mental activity feels like, the better you'll be able to recognize other subtle inputs.

Second, recognize the ring of truth. When Spirit speaks to you, deep in your core it feels right. You don't need to question that. Go with it. This is not the same as hearing an idea that accords with your beliefs. In the personality world we often think something is right just because it is similar to a belief or opinion we already have in our mental bodies. This is the sort of 'truth' that sets people to nodding their heads vigorously to show they support an idea. But the real ring of truth happens when the information resonates deeply in our core as valid and correct, even if it goes against something we would like to believe. When we receive guidance from spirit, it always has this deep ring of truth.

Third, feel the location of the input or words in your field. If the location is out in front of your head somewhere, the message is coming from your own mind or a dark energy trying to pass itself off as your higher self. However, if you feel the location of the input deep in your core, you know it's coming through your own fields from your own higher energies.

Finally, always remember that your higher self will never speak in unkind or negative terms. Spirit is always unconditionally accepting and supportive of its personality. Most people normally hear nasty or unkind voices in their heads, criticizing and aggressively undermining their own hopes and actions. These nasty voices represent dark consciousness that has gotten lodged in the person's field. They should never be mistaken for the voices of the higher self or spirit guidance. In the next chapter I will explain what these dark energies are and how to work with them.

In general, our higher energies are as eager to communicate with us as we are to hear from them. There is no hierarchy of importance or status, and you're not 'bothering' anyone by staying in connection with your own higher dimensions. It's important not to feel inferior or the guiding process can be undermined. As spiritual beings, we need the personality to explore what's possible in the physical dimension. The spiritual self wants to get information and advice through to the personality self, and is engaged whenever the smaller self will listen. Therefore, when you have a communications channel set up, make good use of it. Suppose you ask a question and get an answer. Well then, go on and ask the following question, and the one after that. If you have a problem with part of the guidance, say so. Engage in a full dialogue. Suppose you're asking whether it's right to go into gardening and the answer is that it's partly right. Go on and ask what part is right. Suppose the answer is that gardening for yourself is right, but gardening for other people is not in your highest good. You realize the urge you've been feeling is to be in your own garden and you really don't feel like going into business as a landscape gardener. This feels right to you in the channeling and you accept it. But it leads to the next question.

You still wonder if you could earn income from something related to gardening. Suppose the suggestion comes back that you could work part-time for someone else, but not open a business of your own. Or, you could make some money selling produce from your own garden. All this comes in as a stream of interaction between your personality and your higher energies. Your spirit self knows that staying in touch with the Earth is important for your human self and gardening helps keep you grounded and healthy. But your spirit also knows that something else is calling to you for your new work and it just isn't obvious yet. Now if the channel still feels open and clear you can also go on to ask about a completely different topic. However, you may have shut it down as you went into thinking about who to work for or whether you want to sell produce or not. If so, it may be better to wait for another time to ask more.

A good rule for developing your spiritual channel is to obey the advice. Input that comes from your own higher energies is in alignment with everything about you and all life everywhere. This is a better base for decision making that the limited world view of the personality mind. If you decide instead to go against the guidance and open a gardening business anyway, you're likely to struggle. It isn't really good for you and you knew that during the channeling. Obeying your guidance is important. Once you've engaged with your spirit energies, you've asked them to be active in your life. If you throw out their guidance, it's as though you're not really serious about working with them. This can make it harder to connect later on. If you obey your guidance, two things will happen. First, you will be guided to choices that are always in your highest good. Second, you'll hone your listening skills so you become more finely tuned as a receptor for spiritual input.

Practicing on small things helps you develop your receptive and interpretive abilities so when there's something important that spirit wants to get through to you, you'll recognize it. I recommend practicing with unimportant parts of life. Try getting in your spiritual stream before going to the grocery store and letting your guidance show you which foods to buy. Of course you should also buy what you know you need from your personality level. Spirit is not intended to replace the personality, but to augment it. I also like to have spirit pick my driving route through town. There are always lots of different routes I could take to get somewhere. I let spirit direct which way to go and I obey. There is no way to 'prove' I was better following the guidance since there's no alternate experience in which another car goes another way. But I always enjoy my drive. I might see a flock of birds or an old tree I haven't noticed before. I might sail clear through a lot of green lights, or by-pass a traffic jam. Sometimes when I'm rushing and need to slow down, it feels as though spirit purposely takes me into a series of red lights to get me to give up my attachment to getting somewhere by a certain time. When I eventually arrive, I'll often find it's a good thing I'm a bit late anyway. By honing the receptive skills of listening and obeying, it becomes easier to recognize unasked for guidance. If you are always open to receive input, spirit can help to guide you to things you wouldn't otherwise have found.

Being open to receive input from spirit at all times can pay off in big ways. One day many years ago I was driving to breakfast with a friend when my guidance was suddenly very insistent that I turn into a car dealership. I'd never been to a dealership before, but the guidance was intense. Always obedient to spirit, I visited the showroom, only to discover the new car I'd been fantasizing about was there, and it was the last day of a significant sale. With great delight I discovered I was able to afford the car that had seemed like only a dream. Spirit knew to take me to the place where I could discover what was possible. Had I ignored the guidance, I would have missed the low price and not been able to afford the car. Another time I was awakened on a snowy February morning with an intense need to buy my son a new mountain bike. He didn't need one until the spring, but the call from guidance was unmistakable. By the afternoon we found ourselves in the local store comparing bikes within our budget. Suddenly the owner announced that for the amount of money we had, he could let us have a sample bike he had in the back. He brought out a one-of-a-kind new model worth easily twice what we had to spend. The owner said "It's a good thing you arrived when you did. I was planning on closing up early today to return this bike to the manufacturer." Again, had I overlooked or ignored the directives from my guidance, we would have missed out on a great deal.

Ultimately, remember that your Higher Self and Spirit Guides will *never* speak in unkind or negative terms. When your personality speaks, it is often related to fears and anxieties. The ideas can be dense and dark and make you feel uncomfortable. However, the higher dimensions will always feel comfortable and peaceful. The content of what they say will *always* be loving and their delivery to you will always be given lovingly. If you hear a voice that speaks in terms of punishment or vengeance or fear or shame or blame, you are talking to a dark energy. Stop immediately. Come back into your heart. Reconnect with your higher energies and ask for assistance. Acknowledge there is dark consciousness in your field and do not assume your higher self is telling you dark things. Spirit is always totally loving. This is an absolute.

Chapter Eight

Demystifying the Dark

In order to know how to live with full awareness of our energetic nature, we need to know something about dark energy. This is a vast and complex subject, certainly better suited to a whole book than just a chapter, but since it is important, I include this brief and somewhat simplified overview. Let me make it clear that by the term 'dark energy' I am not referring to some sinister force of evil; nor am I suggesting some version of black magic. While these are specific uses of dark energy, they are not part of our day-to-day relationship with the dark. Part of the problem we humans have in being willing to learn about the dark is that we fear the entire topic and condemn it as sinister or evil. We're afraid to examine it at all in case it 'gets us'. This projection onto the dark gives it way too much power and prevents us from developing a natural and wise relationship with it. I'm also not talking about the destructive force of nature, the Black Madonna, or the Destroyer. I see the Destroyer energy as the great recycler of the universe, reducing structure to its component parts to be reused in a new creation. It is not 'dark' in the sense I'm working with here.

What I do mean by 'dark energy' is consciousness that has no light or love in it. This unloving consciousness can be found within us or outside of us. There can be darkened emotions as part of our human material in our own personal stream of consciousness. There can also be darkness that is part of a ray of dark consciousness that streams from the Divine Source in its own exploration. In most negative human experiences, there is an overlap, where the external dark ray has become embedded within the natural human experience. It is important that we learn to tell the difference between these two sources of negative experience and not claim both as part of our human nature.

Darkness is by definition the absence of light and love. Let's use a physical example to make the idea of an 'absence' clear. Think for a moment of an artist making a sculpture. Sometimes the artist makes a hole in the clay as part of the design. The hole exists as an absence of the clay but part of the creative expression of the artist. If the hole is filled in, the absence no longer exists. The way the hole is delineated is by a clear boundary or edge at which there is no more clay. The hole has no source of its own except the clay surrounding it. The same is true of dark consciousness. Darkness exists as an absence of love and light but part of the expression of the Creator. In the sculpture, if the clay is replaced, the hole no longer exists; and in the universe, if the love or light is returned, the darkness no longer exists. Turn a light on in the darkest room and the darkness just blinks out of existence. It has no source of its own other than the light. Bring love to any moment of suffering and the suffering vanishes. Darkness relies on love for its existence.

Personal dark is our own lack of love in our human experience. The ray of dark consciousness is outside us, following its own journey through time and space. But because they are both dark, the personal gets into relationship with the external. It is in these unrecognized relationships that we suffer greatly. However, as with any relationship, if we understand what we have agreed to and what we actually want, we can take charge of our experience and build a healthy relationship. Darkness is here for a reason and when we make use of it within its own parameters, we can benefit from the experience. What the darkness does is point us directly to a part of ourselves that needs love. If we learn to follow its direction, we can find and heal all the hurting aspects of our selves. The result is that we clear the dark consciousness from our fields and live a much more enlightened and loving human experience.

Any relationship is a two-way street though, so there must be something the darkness gets in return from us. What dark consciousness wants is access to the physical dimension. The dark can't build a body since it can't come in contact with atoms that are made of light. But the physical dimension is a very interesting place to explore; so dark consciousness wants to get inside someone else's body to have physical experience. In effect, it seeks to experience the physical world through a host. We allow it to enter our energy fields and it explores physical life through us, through negative behaviour. The dark can be thought of as a parasite. In a moment of need it offers us help and we accept. It then jumps into our field and takes up residence so to speak. It can't help us, but now we're stuck with it. It takes careful attention to tell the difference between this foreign dark stream and our own inner suffering, but once a person gets the hang of it, it becomes much easier to deny access to the dark and to clear old dark from our fields.

If we're actually hosting the dark, then some very important questions arise. Why do we let the dark into our fields in the first place? What do we think it will do for us? What actually happens when the dark lives through us? How do we get the love we need if there's dark in the way? And how do we clear the dark out of our fields again? In the remainder of this chapter I will begin to answer these questions. Whether you accept these ideas as fact or metaphor doesn't really matter. Interacting with dark consciousness as if these ideas are valid will provide you with powerful tools for avoiding negative experiences, healing negative habits and transforming limiting beliefs.

Personal Dark

The human emotional spectrum runs from delightful to awful, from ecstacy to terror. Through our emotional bodies, we each have access to the whole range of different emotions including the best and worst.

We may prefer some emotional states over others and choose to access our favorites more often, but we all know them all. Emotions are important. They provide input for our learning and growth. In a good state of being, we aim for what delights us and avoid things that make us feel bad. Emotions provide feedback on the experiences of our lives. If something makes us feel positive emotions, we orient to doing more of it, and if something makes us feel negatively, we steer away from it. Emotional feedback is a crucial aspect of the human design. It is our own natural condition and we do it on our own. We don't need help from spirit to feel good when life delights us, and we don't need the dark to make us suffer when things go wrong.

Whenever we have an experience that includes a negative emotional reaction, our emotional field contracts and becomes denser. Through becoming denser, it also darkens. This is our own personal dark action, occurring totally within our own energy field. If the event is more than a passing moment, our mental body will interpret the negative experience and offer explanations for it. Suppose we feel naturally angry because a co-worker betrayed us. We might naturally say "I was an idiot to have trusted him." Or suppose we feel naturally unhappy when a lover ends a relationship. We might say "I feel I'm not good enough." These reactions are negative, but natural. Taken by themselves, they don't reflect dark consciousness but only a darkened aspect of our own personal consciousness.

The solution to our agony is always to connect with love. Love helps us see that the co-worker was lying and we couldn't have seen it coming. Or, love helps us remember that we're more than good enough and very lovable. The love can come directly from spirit on the inside or through a loving friend on the outside. Either way, love is always the balm that dissolves our negative feelings. So, personal dark exists as a natural function of human life and points us to an aspect of ourselves that needs love. The dark is a place without love or light in our own fields, just as it is in cosmic terms. By restoring the love, the suffering stops.

Dark Consciousness

The larger external ray of dark consciousness streams from the Divine Source. Its expression is the lack of love and light. It probably exists in every dimension, exploring life in all forms from a non-loving perspective. Maybe God created this dark ray to enable explorations of love. If love couldn't be removed, then it wouldn't be possible to feel its power, or to feel how much we like and need it. Maybe we need the contrast to explore the depths of love. Like a happy young person setting out on an adventure, we choose to leave the wonder of omnipresent love to go exploring and creating. We choose to challenge ourselves to learn both easy and hard lessons. If a moment comes when all life collectively decides we've explored enough with the dark ray, then we'll probably close it from the God-side. But as long as it's still useful to us, we'll continue experiencing it.

What is the process through which dark energy and human consciousness interact? The possibility for engaging with new dark happens in that moment when the human emotional field contracts and becomes denser and darker. Since like attracts like, as the field darkens, it attracts dark consciousness toward it. The dark is drawn toward the edge of the person's energy field. Recall that the dark is seeking a human host so it can explore life in the physical dimension. Now a negotiation begins. The dark would like a chance to live through the person and the person needs loving help. In order to gain access to the person's field, the dark has to convince the person it can help. It begins to speak, offering to do something the person needs, like protect or empower or befriend them. The human is grateful someone came along to help and doesn't realize the help is being offered by dark consciousness. The person believes the voice can help and by accepting the offer, allows the dark to enter their field.

In the moment the dark enters the person's field, a contract is entered into between the two, like landlord and tenant. The human gives the dark a place to live and the dark gives the human companionship of some kind. The obvious problem though is that the dark is loveless, so it can't actually help the person to feel better. Its style of companionship is to bully and criticize. All it does is sit in the hole where the need for love exists without actually providing anything good. For the human this means the need stays unmet and the negative feeling stays active. In fact, for the human, the situation is now considerably worse than it was before accepting the offer of 'help'. The person now has the original wound, still unmet, as well as dark consciousness that can only make him or her feel worse.

From the dark's perspective, it has gained access to the human field and therefore to the human psyche and behaviour. It's now able to explore what it's like to be in the physical world through the person. It does so through offering and encouraging negative thoughts, words and actions. It requires the person to continue feeling the darker emotions since it needs the dark hole to live in. If the person actually revisits the original need and gets connected with love, the dark can no longer stay. It either dissolves into the light or jumps out of the person's field. So for its own self-preservation and purpose, the dark needs the human to continue feeling bad.

To keep the human feeling bad, the dark 'converses' with us. It talks inside our heads. It says unkind and unsupportive things like "You can't do that! Who do you think you are? You don't believe that crap do you? You're just a lowly worm, a useless turd. Look at you! You're stupid, ugly, fat, unworthy and besides, God doesn't love you. You should be ashamed of yourself. Love doesn't exist for you, you moron. It's hopeless. You're screwed." The dark also says unkind and unsupportive things about the external world like "That guy's a jerk. The world sucks. This place is a dump. There's no such thing as love. Look at those people making fools of themselves. What kind of crap is this? They're out to get you. You can't trust anyone." In fact, the voice of the dark is so well recognized that it has made its way into our mythologies and legends. For example, in J. R. R. Tolkein's *The Lord of the Rings*, Smeagol is tortured by the dark consciousness in his field that presents as Gollum. He switches back and forth between listening to his own voice and the voice of the dark.[17] It is human error to mistake the voice of the dark for our own inner voice. It's also a mistake to think of it as our own dark or shadow. Our personal dark is the little hurting hole beneath the visiting dark. Our personal dark needs love, compassion, respect and attention to feel better. Instead it gets a bully who will say anything to make sure it stays hurting.

What's more, the dark speaks aloud from the mouth of its host any time the host allows it. Like channeling any spirit consciousness, the human says the negative thoughts of the dark aloud to others. More often than not, the second person allows the darkness in his or her field to answer, thereby colluding with the first person that the dark perspective is valid. We hear the voice of the dark speaking between people all the time. In this way the dark gets to experience relationship in the physical dimension too. If a person gets really angry and rages at someone, the dark has a hey-day. In fact, when a person is raging it is often possible to see the flash of darkness cross through their eyes as the dark takes over and the person collapses. Afterwards the person might say "I don't know what came over me. It's so unlike me to do something like that." In fact, it was the dark consciousness that took over as the person's hurt exploded, and the person is on the right track to think he or she wouldn't have done such a thing. All negative behaviors are just actions of the dark in the deep wounds of the human. Every negative act points directly to a hurting wound somewhere deep inside.

Looked at this way, the dark can be considered as an unwelcome parasite. It wants into a human energy field to be able to explore the physical dimension. So it hangs around waiting for an opportunity. It takes advantage of a moment of human weakness by seducing the human with offers it can't fulfill. Once it gets what it wants, its own need for self-preservation will keep it hurting its host. The more the host hurts, the better off the dark is. When a wound gets triggered and negative feelings and behaviors result, this is the action of the dark in the physical world. The bigger the hurt, the bigger the effect the dark gets to experience. The worse a person's behaviour, the worse the pain they're hiding. Really bad behaviour indicates a terrible lack of love on the inside.

If a person doesn't feel enough love in general in life, he or she can become depressed by the constant barrage of dark thoughts. There may be love in their lives, but the person can't feel it. None of the nasty thoughts are valid since they're only the self-serving offerings of the dark. But if the person has a lot of dark parasites, the cacophony can be overwhelming. The more depressed the person is, the more the dark gets to experience physical existence. Depression feeds on itself since the more negative a person feels, the more their emotional field contracts and the more new dark they allow in. It's a slippery slope from overwhelm to deep depression. But the more depressed a person is, the less likely they are to look for or to find love. This is equally true of a violent person, or an angry person. The worse the person feels, the more dark they engage with and the worse they feel again. It's a vicious cycle.

There is a simple, but not easy, solution to erase the problems created by the dark. It is to love the self. The only solution is to bring love into the ragged holes underneath the dark parasites, to meet the original needs and heal the wounds with love. Then there is no absence and the dark can't stay. The person breaks his contract with the dark, no longer allowing it access to his field. He evicts the dark through replacing it with the love of the higher energies. The dark is disgruntled because it loses its (un)happy home, but it has to go. The love will eradicate it otherwise. Sometimes dark parasites choose to be touched by the light and to dissolve, but more often they jump back out of the field again to avoid the love. Often they leave calling back "You'll be sorry! You can't get along without me! I'm the only thing keeping you safe, or likable, or sane you know!" If the person has a moment of weakness and believes the parasite, even for an instant, it jumps back into his field and the clearing has to begin all over again. The weak link of the human is in believing the words of the dark.

The Human-Dark Relationship

So let's summarize this relationship we have with the dark. First we don't recognize the dark as a separate stream of consciousness. We don't notice when we hear it or see it or sense it. We aren't aware of it making its offers, so we don't realize when we've let it in to our fields. Once it's inside, we think of it as part of ourselves, calling it shadow and claiming it as our own inner self. We confuse its inner voice with our own. We relate to it as a valid part of ourselves. We accept advice from it and think and act in accord with it. We believe negative things about ourselves and other people based on its input. Then we let it act through us when we feel upset.

We don't realize we've let the dark in to our fields and we want to deny its existence. Often we refuse to take responsibility for our bad actions, feeling insulted if someone implies we're the sort of person who would do such a thing. Or, if we do admit we did the bad act, we justify our actions through blaming someone else or some set of circumstances. Or, if we do fully take responsibility and actually work to change our behaviour, we still don't heal the wound and clear the dark from our field. Although we don't let the dark act through us any more, we're still stuck listening to it on the inside. This is an improvement because we've made changes in our outer behaviour, but problematic because the dark still eats away at us, making us feel bad about ourselves and making us judge silently, regardless of how we act.

On the outside, we fear the dark. We fear talking about it or giving it any attention. We believe it's somehow out to get us. We realize it can hurt us, but we don't realize it can only function through a hurting human. We mistakenly think it can hurt us all on its own. We think we're at its mercy, powerless to stop it, so we don't confront it or say no to it. At the same time, we think the dark is valid. We justify its existence. Maybe because our planet spins and we get half a day of light and half of dark, we give the dark credit for half of all reality. We buy in to the notion of the ying-yang symbol, assigning the dark the right to dominate half of our thinking, actions and beliefs. Just because there is a duality in physical nature that opposes things like up and down, we buy in to the idea that half of everything must be dark. Instead of seeing all the colors of the universe, and realizing that black is only one of the colors, we give it credit for half of all reality. Then we empower it by thinking we need it, that it justifies some purpose, confusing dark consciousness with our own natural negative feedback signals. Finally we glorify it. We glorify it in our culture through such things as Star Wars or gangster movies. We glorify it in our religions through a punishing God or wrathful deities. We glorify it in our educational systems by giving status to fear-provoking authority. We glorify it through our militaristic systems of power-over and oppression. And we glorify it in our economic systems through accepting excess profits and hostile takeovers. So we're in a relationship with the dark in which we allow it, enable it, hide it, fear it, deny it, justify it and glorify it.

The Solution

So, what is the solution to this unpleasant condition we find ourselves in? The solution is always to connect with love. Love can always be found in the monadic field and brought through to the needs of the moment, even if it isn't obviously available in the physical scene. Love is always here, within us and around us, if we only remember to connect with it. Love is accessible during a moment of pain or anguish, if we only remember to call to it. Love can be accessed through our higher selves and spiritual helpers, if we only remember to ask for it. We have language that suggests it to ourselves—"Oh my God! Saints above! Heaven help us! Jesus Christ!"—but we seem to have forgotten what we're actually trying to do with our words. We don't need to sit all alone, waiting for the dark to meet our misery. The love is right here, just waiting to help.

We can also use love to heal the long-ago pains and clear the old dark from our fields. If we can revisit the old story and bring love to ourselves in it, we usurp the dark from its position and replace its 'help' with true help. The hole is filled and the need is truly met. We feel loved, lovable, safe and comforted. And we see that the dark didn't live up to its promise. In fact, it made things worse. Then we can break our contract with the dark and evict it from our fields. This is a straightforward act. If you worked for a company that had a bad supplier who didn't meet commitments or deadlines and provided a useless product, you wouldn't have any trouble breaking your contract and severing your relationship. This is exactly the same model to use with the dark. It isn't doing what it said it would do and it makes you feel worse. So in essence, you choose to get your needs met by a different supplier, the light, and you break your contract with the old supplier, the dark. You aren't just asking them to go away; you are replacing them with something that can truly meet your needs.

Practical Exercises

- *Recognizing Dark Consciousness*

The first thing to learn is to recognize the voice and energetic template of the dark; to stop thinking of it as part of yourself, or part of the person you hear it speaking through. Since the dark is a one-trick pony it always says the same sort of thing, so it's easy to recognize. It is unloving and unkind and usually speaks in a critical or bossy or cynical voice inside your head. A strong clue that the voice belongs to a parasite of dark energy is that it almost always speaks in the third person, referring to you as 'you'. It says things like "You can't do that, You're an idiot, You don't believe that do you? You're not safe here, or You can't trust anyone." Referring in this way to you as 'you' is a sure sign it's the voice of the dark. Occasionally the dark pretends to be the light and speaks in soft tones, but the underlying message is still that you aren't really capable or strong or loved or safe, that you should be afraid, and the feeling is that it is somehow 'helping' you.

It's easy to tell the voice of the dark apart from the voice of your higher self or guides because they are totally loving and unconditionally supportive and want you to grow to be the best and most empowered version of yourself possible. They support you directly with love. Their answers feel like spiritual experiences. The dark is the opposite, always trying to keep you small and imprisoned in fear and unworthiness. It keeps reminding you of your weaknesses and past mistakes, shaming you or keeping you hesitant and limited. So the first and most crucial step is to recognize dark consciousness.

The second important thing to learn is to stop talking to the dark and stop listening to its 'advice.' It will keep talking as long as you're listening. It's exactly like phone solicitors who want to sell you a cruise or get you to donate to a charity. As long as you keep listening, they keep talking. But if you hang up, they have no ear to talk to. So it is with the dark. You have to hang up on it, to become unavailable to it. The less you pay attention to it, and the more often you challenge its beliefs with love, the less interested it will be in talking to you.

The third step is to pay attention when something is going wrong in your life and to connect purposefully with love. If you can connect with your higher energies to get your needs met, you won't be in a vulnerable position and open to the dark. Even if you have a hard time feeling connected to your higher energies, you can at least recognize the voice and the template of the dark as it comes to offer its 'help' and be wise enough to say 'No'. As soon as you can, connect with love through your higher energies or a loving friend and get your inner needs met. And if you hear yourself swearing, it's probably a good indication that you want to connect with the light and love of your higher self.

- *Breaking Contracts with the Dark*

Clearing old dark from your field is more complicated and involves healing tools and skills. The processes are too complex to do justice to here. However, the idea is that you can dialogue with the dark consciousness in the place that is hurting, and if you instruct it to, the dark will show you the moment it first entered your field. You can then revisit that original story, connect with your Higher Self in the context of the old story and get your original needs met with love. Once your needs are truly being met by love, you can break your contract with the dark and it will clear from your field.

Once all or most of the dark is cleared from your energy fields, you may still feel naturally sad or worried or angry from time to time. These are the normal states of human experience and don't indicate the presence of dark consciousness. The negative emotions are doing their job, giving you feedback to help you understand something about your life. You may need to be careful in those moments not to contract with new dark again, or to call up soul level dark beliefs again. If you can always remember to connect with your own higher energies, there will always be love for you to help you through your challenging moment. And if you've gotten good at recognizing the voice of the dark and knowing with certainty it's lying to you, you need never be tempted by it again. The best answer to any temptation of the dark is "There's nothing you can offer me that I need or want. There's nothing you can offer me that I can't get from the light". After all, anything the dark can do, the light can certainly do better.

Chapter Nine

Putting It All Together— Self-Realization

Let us take a moment to review all we have covered so far. I began with an invitation to recognize yourself as a stream of consciousness, gifted with the raw materials of body, emotion, thought and something else. Then I proposed that you already spend those raw materials in your moment-by-moment choices of what to make matter in your world. I then suggested that there is a much larger set of choices available than most people know about and provided details about the nonphysical dimensions of our human experience. I included some simple exercises to help you develop some skills of energy awareness. Next I suggested that it is possible and desirable for the different parts of the self to communicate with each other and to ask for and accept guidance and direction from within. Finally I explained the nature of dark energy in order to bring our relationship with negativity within the choice set as well.

If this information I have provided is akin to an alphabet, I want now to ask what kinds of words and stories we can create with it. I invite you to explore and generate from this new material in whatever way you can imagine. To get you started, I'd like to propose three different aspects of life that this information can be applied to. The three are self-realization, personal healing and spiritual enlightenment. I will consider each of these in detail in the remaining chapters of the book. While it is possible to examine these as separate ways of integrating this information into real life, it isn't so obvious that they are actually so separable. However, as a starting point let's consider them as separable units.

To evolve from being a personality-driven human to being a spiritually inspired person is a long journey. The first stages are all about the personality and the soul beginning to dialogue in an open and ongoing way. After the personality resonates and embodies the soul nature, then the person is ready to begin really aligning with his or her spiritual nature. The process of soul-realization is well served by the nature of the personality and soul fields. Spiritual enlightenment and a compassionate relationship with humanity come from integrating the monadic and higher energy fields into both the personality and the soul. In this chapter we explore the processes of soul-realization. In later chapters we will progress through healing to spiritual enlightenment and embodiment in the human world.

Self-Realization through Self-Awareness

Each human is the embodiment of a soul that seeks to express itself in the physical world. It is the important job of the personality to facilitate this process. If a personality is in good contact with its spirit and soul, the journey can be realized well. But if the personality is busy trying to become someone that isn't representative of the soul, there will be friction and unhappiness within, and disease or disorder in the body. Self-realization is the process through which the soul is made real in the flesh. It allows the soul to materialize in the physical plane. It makes the soul matter. The process of bringing energetic awareness to the self is not meant as an end in itself, but as a means for discovering and embodying the soul more fully, to turn up in the world as a freer, more creative agent.

In common life it is often difficult for the personality to hear the voices of its soul or spirit, to differentiate them from the cacophony of voices of people, media and the dark. However, applying the simple skills of energy awareness to the process allows the soul to be known and recognized more easily. Allowing the soul to make decisions instead of the mind doing so leads a person to manifesting more and more soul in their lived world. By paying attention to the subtle indicators of the energy fields, a person brings a deeper sense of awareness to the processes of self-realization. Bringing awareness to the subtle shifts in energy experiences brings a higher degree of self-awareness. Watching for and noticing subtle shifts in the energy fields can provide important information about how the self is getting along in the world. This is really an argument for becoming highly tuned to the self, as a way of becoming more self-realized.

By knowing what's right for us on the inside, we become better citizens of life, better tuned to understanding what's going on, and with a stronger, more empowered ability to create and manifest in our outer world. Becoming self-realized in this way allows us to turn up with a more open heart and clearer mind in the world beyond the self. A person whose soul is engaged in his personal journey becomes a more fully activated citizen. His own self-realization flows out into the collective, enabling everyone to become more creative, capable agents in the social fabric.

Noticing

So, how does one use the information in this book to become more fully realized in the world? The first step is by noticing what's happening in an ongoing way. Notice when something makes you feel good and when something makes you feel bad. Your physical body might give you clues by relaxing deeply, or becoming tight and painful. Your breathing might change. Your emotional body might give you clues by expanding or contracting in response to thoughts or experiences. You might feel like crying for no obvious reason. Your mental body might give you clues by reminding you of something you lived through in the past that seems similar to the current situation, or you might hear yourself repeating a certain phrase over and over.

Developing a high level of self-awareness is about becoming highly attuned to the subtle indicators that go on all the time in your subtle bodies. The location of the shift gives you information about how it is affecting you. Each chakra responds in accord with its domain in your life. A movement in your heart points to how you feel about love, trust or hope. A movement in your solar plexus addresses how you feel about yourself. A movement in the throat indicates something about your experience of expressing into the shared world.

Suppose you're feeling fine, in a conversation with a good friend, when you suddenly notice that your heart chakra is contracting and your solar plexus is tightening in response to something she said. It's a good idea to take the time to go back over her words to discover what the underlying reason for your reaction was. Suppose you explore within yourself and discover that what she said made you feel rejected and unloved. Then you might choose to do healing work within yourself to heal an old pain, and you might choose to talk with your friend about it. You might want to know what was going on in her reality that made her say whatever it was that triggered you, to feel more deeply whether it was appropriate to feel emotional or not. Was she actually intending to give you a message or not? She might have been intending to pull back a bit from your relationship because she has a new friend she's spending a lot of time with. In this case your reaction is reasonable, although you might still choose to help yourself reduce the pain of your response. Or she might have meant nothing of the sort, but was feeling stressed, thinking about how to manage fitting an event with you into her overcrowded schedule and you were fully mistaken in her intention. This ability to observe and discover your own inner truth will reduce emotional outbursts and enable you to know yourself much better. All behaviors stay possible, but you have a deeper sense of what's real for you and why you are choosing your option.

Living with this sort of self-awareness is helpful to those around you as well as to yourself. Imagine if it were you who had said the words and your friend who had the reaction. It would be much more comfortable for you if she told you how she felt and why rather than suddenly flying off in an emotional reaction. This sort of self-awareness leads to less conflict, blaming and confusion in the world. The ability to know your inner reality offers an opportunity to engage with other people in a more honest and fruitful way. Personal awareness helps bring clarity and compassion to your relationships with the rest of the world.

The emotional body has a very important job to do in the human continuum. It lets us know how we feel about things. It directs us toward people and situations we like and away from ones we dislike. It keeps us away from physical danger by warning us if we are at risk of being harmed. Used as a beacon, it can lead us toward the passions of our souls and away from things we feel duty-bound to care about. It can also guide us toward old wounds that need loving attention.

Suppose that you begin tuning in to your emotional body and discover that every single day when you go to work, you feel depressed and unhappy. This is probably feedback from your soul telling you to find another job. Or suppose you realize that every single time you have to engage with your father-in-law, you end up feeling chastised and humiliated. This may be an indication from your soul that you should consider avoiding contact with the man as much as possible. Or suppose you cry with joy and delight every single time you see a horse or think about going riding. Then your soul is calling to you to spend some time with horses. Such messages from your emotional body can be used to direct your explorations in life. If we follow the things that make our hearts sing and avoid the ones that make us cringe, chances are we will live a more fulfilled life.

An emotional reaction can also be an indication of an old wound buried deep inside. Maybe you know that your father-in-law is really a good man who loves you dearly, but his demeanor reminds you strongly of your own father who was cruel. Your emotional reaction might be guiding you not to avoiding your father-in-law but to healing your buried wounds. In this case, by noticing and questioning how you feel, you would be led to the activity of healing. Either way, the emotional body is guiding you towards something that is good for you. It is important to notice all reactions, including things that repulse you or that you find boring. These reactions might be the faces of old wounds guiding you toward aspects of your life that need help. Or they can be messages from your soul to guide you away from things that won't feed your growth this time around.

I'm reminded of a couple I know who chose not to have children. They both had strong emotional reactions to the idea. At first they thought they would have a family, but as the years passed without deciding it was time to start, they began to look into their deeper feelings. Each one worked through old beliefs and found places where they felt guilty if they didn't have children. They each healed the underlying wounds that harbored the guilt. When they had both walked the healing journey fully and knew their reactions were not stemming from old wounds or unmet needs, it became clear they really didn't want to have children. It was right for them to express themselves in other ways in this lifetime. They became social activists of a high order and have gone on to help tens of thousands more children than they ever could have touched in a traditional family unit.

It is critically important not to become judgmental or moralistic about the choices people make when they are following their soul's calling. When this couple realized it wasn't right for them to have children, their decision stirred up indignation among people in their lives who thought they knew better what was right for the couple. But if we each seek to be fully self-realized, then we must accept and support each other in the same journey. What's right for one is not right for another. This is the beauty and the creative gift of mankind. I know many people who woke up to their soul's journeys and quickly left the unloving atmosphere of the corporate world. However, I know another woman who switched from being a highly gifted healer to working for a big corporation as her soul directed her to taking on tasks of a different kind. She needed to develop her confidence in relation to the bigger world. She faced some ridicule and aggression from others in the 'spiritual' world for 'selling-out' as they saw it. But for her it was a clear call to develop a different part of herself. It isn't the action itself that matters but what part of our self is engaged with the acting.

To become a self-realized being it is necessary for us to explore our talents and passions. We find our way to these through noticing our curiosities and investigating what draws us in. Sometimes there is a soul-calling that is heard in childhood and stays with us always. I am reminded of a young boy I knew who loved the weather. He was very knowledgeable about clouds and sun as a child and he went on to become an expert meteorologist in his adult years. For whatever reasons, his soul called him to studying weather patterns from an early age and he listened. More often though, as time progresses, the soul evolves and our interests change dramatically. A person goes from being a teacher to becoming a volunteer in Africa to studying photography to writing a book about orphans. As time progresses, so does the discovery of self. As a culture we seem willing to accept this sort of evolution if it takes place slowly and each episode lasts for a long time. But we seem less tolerant if the person evolves rapidly through the explorations. It is a mistake to think that just because we once felt a certain way about something that we have to continue feeling like that, or to moralize about other people being fickle or not steadfast. The soul needs lots of room to grow; and a life is a very long time.

To begin to bring this quality of self-awareness into everyday life one main approach is to take the time to go within and notice how you really feel about things. Slow down and ask how you actually feel. Stay connected to the subtle sensations of your emotional body and your chakras. When the process of decision-making is slowed down in this way, it gives us time to notice more of what's going on and the opportunity to check things out. When we spend money we usually take some care in making a choice. But when we spend the raw material of our consciousness we all too often jump from one reaction to the next. By staying connected with the energy fields and aware of the subtle flow of information they provide, we can take more care in our spending, and get more value from our choices.

Exploring

A more pro-active way to integrate the skills of energy awareness moves beyond merely noticing what's happening to purposely exploring how you feel about certain topics. It's possible to go digging within and discover your own belief systems and paradigms. Question everything and find out how you really feel about it all. When you discover you have a belief about something, assume you're wrong, and that you don't know what the truth is. Through this process of not knowing, you create an opening for life to reveal itself. By bringing attention to your beliefs in this way you can notice how your beliefs and opinions drive your behaviour and choices. You may be out of balance in your life as a result of these implicit paradigms. Through the discovery process you may decide the belief outlived its usefulness long ago, or you may realize it is a good, strong part of you that you wish to keep or even strengthen. Through this sort of observation and exploration process, it's possible to discover what your inner motivations and intentions really are.

For example, I used to think that being a good mother meant I had to produce a made-from-scratch, sit-down dinner for my children every night. As a fully-employed single mother of four this was a huge undertaking that often left me feeling stressed and grumpy. The ability to find and explore my beliefs stemmed from observing my behaviour and how I felt about it. I followed the patterns of stress in my body to the locations where I held the hidden beliefs. In this case just discovering the belief was enough to let it change without deeper healing work. Once my 'good mothering' was no longer tied to cooking I became free to meet our nutritional and social needs through a much wider set of options.

Through exploring self-awareness in this way, the over-blown role most of us give to our minds can become apparent. Most normal thought is repetitive, self-defending and not really very interesting. If you bring awareness to the patterns of your thoughts, to knowing your own habits both good and bad, you will gain insight about yourself. You will discover how you grew to be the way you are, what makes you accept or reject new information, what your defenses are, who you discriminate for or against and so on. Bringing awareness to the functioning of your mental body as an energy field rather than as your self-identity will free you to explore new ways that might fit you better and allow you to become more highly realized in your life. As you explore the limitations of normal thought you open more to the workings of the higher mind. Ultimately the mind needs to be brought into balance with the heart and the higher self. The mind is a very good tool, but it isn't the master. Bringing awareness to the processes of the mind helps us to see the true relationship between the serving mind and the more subtle inner mastery. The more the mind takes a back seat to the higher self, the more evolved the mind will become. Bringing a high level of awareness to the functioning of the mind will help you to uncover the mechanisms of this process.

Another good place for exploration is in nightly dreams. Many people make use of their dreams as material for investigating their lives. Bringing a heightened awareness of the energy fields into dream analysis can lead to interesting new insights. The entire dream is happening in the subtle fields. Bringing awareness to the dream as a subtle instruction can be helpful. There are many ways to integrate energy awareness into dream analysis but the most straightforward is to stay aware and notice how your energy field responds to aspects of the dream as you think about it later.

I remember a dream in which a bottle of oil spilled and dripped to the floor. As I worked the dream later, I felt into the oil and it pointed me toward a dark energy in my solar plexus that was a critical part of the message of the dream. Had I not been aware to follow how the dream affected my energy field, I would not have found my way to this insight, nor cleared the dark energy at that time. In general, any noticing of dark energy or exploring that reveals dark consciousness somewhere in your field is an opportunity to clear it. The more chances we make and take to disempower dark consciousness from our fields, the better we will feel and the more positive our contribution will be to our lives and the world around us. Always remember, undetected is uncorrected.

Another way to analyze the energetic content of dreams is to move the point of awareness of the dreaming self around the scene. Just as you can move your point of awareness around your body and energy field, so can you move your point of awareness around a dreamscape. Information can then be received from various parts of the dream, just as in the earlier example about receiving a message from a bird. As you move the dreamer's awareness into the image, a sense of what the object represents will emerge. For example, I remember a dream of riding a bus with a happy driver and a yappy dog. Moving my consciousness around into different players in the dream image afterwards, I 'received' information: the bus was my journey; the driver was my higher self; and the yappy little dog was my fears.

Experimenting

From noticing and exploring how we feel about aspects of our lives, it is a natural step to experimenting with new approaches or beliefs. Life is made of constant change, so you might as well change consciously and on purpose. If you base your changes on callings of your soul and spirit as well as media, friends and family, you will begin to feel more engaged with your life, and the changes you make will bring more positive results. Whenever the personality acts in alignment with its soul and spirit, good things happen. Occasionally something really bombs, but that too can be great feedback. The more we trust the process, the more we learn to go with the flow and accept and integrate all that comes from spirit.

Suppose you've been dreading an upcoming family event but assuming you had to go anyway. You might experiment with not going and see what happens. You don't really know how you or others will feel and behave until you give life a chance to show you. It might end up not being such a big deal to others after all, and you can relax your worries about always having to be there. Or they might get so angry that you realize the only reason you've been going all these years is to avoid getting yelled at, and that as an adult, this isn't a good enough reason any more. Then you might need to talk with the others and set some new parameters around what you're willing to tolerate from them. As long as you stay engaged and communicative with your higher energies, the end result will be better for you than the original condition.

It is good to stay connected with the higher energies as much of the time as possible. If you really practice getting connected and staying connected, it will pay off in big ways. At first it seems awkward and you have to remember both to do it and how to do it, but after it becomes habitual, you can rely on your inner connection for guidance and direction. Then you can ask about things that are going on in your world and experiment with new approaches. The idea here is that as long as you stay in contact with your higher energies and work with advice and guidance, you can try things out and make use of the feedback. Through these processes you can hone and develop yourself, discovering new ways of self-expression that work well for you. This allows life to evolve with the subtle indicators being used for feedback and re-direction. The only thing to watch out for is the experience happening in your core self somewhere and not just out in your third eye chakra.

Another wonderful way to notice, explore and experiment is through art, music or dance. Getting in touch with the subtle self and letting it reveal itself in creative ways is a wonderful process of exploration. Suppose you connect deeply with your higher energies, then begin to dance. Let every movement flow from your spiritual self and feel the results throughout your body. If there's something that's been bothering you, take the time to go visit it and allow the dancing to engage with it. Your movements and rhythms will probably change dramatically as you explore the tensions. Then when the higher energies engage again for healing and insight, your movements will once again become harmonious. New pathways can be laid down as potential solutions for your energetic patterns to follow. You may or may not have emotional catharsis or cognitive realizations. Either way, the dancing will have led you through an experience of self that couldn't have been accessed in any other way. Exploration, discovery, revelation, healing, insight, wisdom; all are accessible through creative means.

You can follow the same sort of process with art or music. Imagine making one drawing, one painting, one poem or one sculpture every day as a way of accessing how you feel beneath the surface of words and concepts. Or play an instrument or sing the depths of your inner sensing as a way of exploring how you really feel about something. I remember once I was driving a long trip alone and to pass the time I began to sing the inner music of each relationship in my life. I went through my family, my children, my friends and my beloved. One by one, I would feel into my inner experience with the person and allow music to well up from inside me that felt just right. There was no need for melody or structure; this was abstract music. As I reflected over the variations, I was deeply intrigued. Some were sweet and simple, others rich and complex. Some revealed themselves as screechy and inharmonious. By allowing myself to move voice and rhythm into the disharmonies, insights were revealed to me about those particular relationships. By allowing the music to unfold, solutions were presented as possibilities for greater harmony with those people. Some of the process involved cognitive thought, but much of it was un-wordable. Overall it was an enlightening process of revelation and healing.

Once you start exploring the self on purpose through energy awareness and experimenting, there are no limits to what you can do. For example, you could explore the inner masculine and inner feminine energies of different parts of your body or different chakras. What are the divine masculine and divine feminine like as they turn up in your field? How do you behave differently in the world as you align with one or the other? Or you could explore the inner child of different energy patterns or chakras, discovering what the talents and passions of those unknown inner kids really are. Maybe in your physical life you weren't able to explore fully, but in your inner world, you are now free to explore and experiment with anything. Ask the inner kids how they feel about things, or what they want you to pay attention to. Let each inner child feel the presence of his or her higher energies directly and you will begin to feel much more stable in your adult life. Or you can explore your introverted chakras and your extroverted ones as specific tools in your world. You may be well developed in the extroverted social self, but feel inadequate and inferior in your introverted places. Or you might feel strong and capable in your introverted solar plexus and third eye, but be very inhibited and stuck in your relational second and throat.

You begin to get the picture here. Once you have begun to make use of your energy fields as tools of daily self-discovery and self-management, you become much more able to know what feels right and good for you, and stronger in the ability to encourage and develop your true self. You will find that many old behaviors transform gently and easily. If they don't, you know how to go looking for the place you're stuck, to bring the healing power of the higher energies to whatever old drama is stored away there. This brings us to the second aspect of life in which the use of energy fields can change life dramatically, and that is the area of healing.

Chapter Ten

Putting it All Together—Healing

We continue with this rather arbitrary division between self-realization and healing although they blend so easily together it is hard to make the distinction. However, there is a subtle difference between the two that is very important. It has to do with purposely connecting with the higher spiritual energies to replace old unhappy beliefs with loving support and spiritual truth. In the last chapter we saw that self-realization can be augmented just by bringing energetic awareness to the experiences of everyday life. A person can gain a lot by noticing, exploring and experimenting with how he or she feels energetically without ever purposefully bringing a higher dimension of self into play. But healing requires connecting with the higher energies. Healing and transformation occur by reconnecting with the love, forgiveness and guiding support of the higher self.

There are different ways a person can integrate energy healing into their own normal life. One is to use healing skills when there is a triggering experience happening. Another is through exploring specific topics that seem stressful or difficult. A third is as a habitual part of life, like an energetic tune-up, or maintenance of the fields. Finally, energy healing skills can be used to help in physical healing of disease or discomforts. It is also possible for therapists and healers of any type to include energetic awareness in the services they offer to others. Let's look at each of these in turn.

Healing when Triggered

The first way to integrate energy healing into regular life occurs when you are in a stressful situation and either are triggered or feel about to get triggered. You may recognize that you are on that slippery slope between feeling fine and feeling really awful. If you can stop your slide towards the edge, you can cross back over the line to feeling good. As soon as you become aware of your energy field reacting to a situation you find yourself in, you can connect with your higher energies. By asking for help and receiving compassion and understanding, you can shift the energy flowing through you and out into the situation. I recall one night talking with a friend on the phone. He began to become emotionally upset about something we were discussing, and I recognized myself going into my own emotional counter-reaction. But instead of sliding into my internal tension, I immediately connected with my higher energies and asked for help. As I did so I was able to see a bigger picture and find a loving approach to our topic. By introducing the higher energies into the discussion, we were able to work out a wise response to the challenge we had uncovered.

Connecting with your higher energies will always help you feel more settled, but sometimes it's not enough to eliminate the whole reaction. Sometimes when you connect you feel slightly better, but still triggered. Then using more directed healing can help greatly, even if you can't get engaged in a lengthy healing process right then. It's beneficial if you can excuse yourself from the situation for a moment. Take a washroom break, or just suggest a short time-out. But even if you can't take a noticeable break, it may still be possible to turn your awareness within to your internal reactions and needs. Once you have this breathing space, move your awareness within and connect with your higher energies. Then move your awareness into the place that is upset, get a sense of what's gotten triggered and ask the higher energies to bring some healing to whatever is going on there. Whatever comes will be good.

I remember a night when I was preparing to give a lecture to a new group. I had presented the material many times to different groups so there was no obvious reason to feel nervous, yet I had a high level of anxiety. Once I noticed that it wasn't going away even though I had re-connected with my higher energies, I stopped my preparations and took a moment to go within. I found the tension in my solar plexus and inside it I discovered an inner child who was terrified of the coming evening. She was certain the new people wouldn't like her. My higher self and I engaged lovingly with her for a few minutes and gave her a chance to check out her fears. She realized that her fears were based on a long ago experience that was really very different. After she felt calmer I suggested that she didn't need to go to the lecture, that there were plenty of adult parts around who could do a good job that night, and she could go play instead. The child self was delighted and ran off to play while the adult self got back to preparing. The anxiety was completely gone and the evening was a great success. The whole healing experience only took a couple of minutes.

Healing is a creative activity. When you invite an energy to open, you never know what's going to come from it. But if the higher energies are really engaged, something good will happen and the result will be a better state than the original one. If you are willing to obey the guidance from your higher self, and if you can stay in a loving relationship with the different aspects of yourself, you will always benefit from the experience. The higher energies will bring more light and love through your field while introducing beliefs that resonate with love. Opening to healing energies while being triggered takes some courage and determination, but it is always a good managerial habit to decrease negative outcomes both for yourself and for others. You are likely to have more peaceful behavior, and there's less likely to be emotional fall-out from passing your dark triggering along the line to someone else.

If you find yourself in a difficult experience with another person who is also on a spiritual healing path, you might agree to call in your higher energies together. Suppose you and your partner find yourselves starting to argue and you start to feel really emotional. You might suggest that you both engage with your higher selves to bring some love and help to the situation. Or you could suggest meditating on the topic, or finding out what spirit has to offer. You could call to a spiritual teacher for advice, or suggest a specific practice you both know. Of course, we are all inclined to find excuses when we're really aggravated, so it's probably wise to wait if you're really in the thick of it. It might be more fruitful to give tempers a chance to settle down before suggesting a call to spirit. This can be helpful to other people too. I remember a time when two of my children were in a fierce fight. One was totally triggered and wildly angry. I had attempted to intervene, but nothing was getting through to the upset one. So I brought out some sweet-grass and smudged them both with some quiet calming words and gestures. The introduction of the higher energies in a form they could recognize enabled them to get past their troubles to a common ground again.

Healing Specific Topics

Energy awareness and healing is a very useful tool for figuring out the underlying nature of difficult issues we face. If the emotional body and the mental body regularly get upset by some normal issue, it indicates there's an underlying pattern causing the distress. Bringing awareness to the location of the discomfort can begin to open the stories and reveal the patterns of thought. Engaging with the higher energies can offer new loving perspectives on the 'truth'. Breaking contracts with old embedded dark can clear the field. The outcome is a more peaceful, loving perspective on life. Through the use of energy healing, reactions to people or triggering situations can be changed for good. Specific habits that limit our lives, including addictions, rigidities or fears can be resolved completely. This style of energy healing can completely clear the residue in the energy field resulting from childhood abuse and other traumas.

To use energy awareness in this way, consider a particular issue and see where the location of distress is. Which chakra or chakras is it in? Suppose you feel annoyed every time you're in the presence of a talkative person, regardless of who it is. You could use energy healing to go inside, identify where you feel the reaction, then move your consciousness into the place of annoyance and feel the emotions there. You might discover deeply buried feelings of unimportance, weakness and unworthiness. Feeling the familiarity of those feelings in that location might take you back into your childhood, to related times of being overruled by older people. Maybe you had older siblings who consistently 'put you down' and ignored you. You could then bring the higher energies through for the child self in those stories and let the child ask if it's true that she's unimportant, weak or unworthy. She will discover directly from the higher energies that these are false beliefs and the truth is one of pure love, unique importance and absolute worth. Once the actual patterns held in the mental body shift fully to the new understandings, that location in your adult field will not get triggered again in the presence of a highly capable person.

Sometimes the triggering doesn't go away entirely with a personality level healing. This can indicate that the same pattern is deeper within, in the patterns of the soul field. If so, the triggering continues but seems somewhat less intense and less personal. It could also indicate the presence of a dark parasite hiding in there. Tracking consciousness into the soul dimension in that same location will open the past life story where the original beliefs were laid down. This story is likely to be a truly traumatic experience, such as death or destruction of some sort. The beliefs will be the same though. Unimportance, weakness and unworthiness will likely feature in the original story.

Perhaps your soul story is as a young prince not normally given authority. For some reason he was allowed to make an important decision, but it went badly and people died as a result. He had to bear the consequences and came to believe he truly was unimportant, weak and unworthy. He let the dark in to help him feel better about himself, but all it did was to remind him constantly of his inabilities compared to other people. To heal this story, the prince connects with his higher energies and gets advice on his decision. Maybe he sees it isn't a good idea, or maybe he's shown it is a fine idea but there are other factors at work that he couldn't have known about. Either way, his higher energies will show him that he is not unimportant, weak or unworthy but totally loved, uniquely important and absolutely worthy. When his beliefs have totally shifted, he can break his contract with the dark that he let in and the dark will have to leave. The result of the healing is that the whole area of both your soul and personality fields will be filled with light and love and the original issue of being upset by capable people will be a distant memory.

Relationships can also be explored energetically. In every combination of two or more people there is an energetic interaction going on. By examining your own energy fields, you can become aware of your contribution to any collective consciousness. To discover your reactions, set up a stimulus and response exercise. First you scan your field as it is on your own, mapping out exactly how you feel in your chakras by yourself. Then begin to think about the other person and feel which chakras change and in what way. Then work your way through your own field, exploring each place that changes and bringing healing to any inner wounds that get triggered. As you change what you bring to the relationship, the relationship itself will transform. Engaging at this level of personal awareness in your relationships will clear your triggers and help you to bring more love and acceptance to the other people in your life.

Energy healing of this style can be applied to any attitudes or issues in your life. You can use this stimulus and response approach to explore your inner patterns about money, sexuality, work, food, or any other issue at all. You can explore specific situations or questions, or more global reactions and responses in your character. You can follow triggers or reactions, or just go fishing on any topic. The opportunities are endless. The result is a deeper and deeper understanding of your true nature and a more and more enlightened ability to embody the higher energies of love.

Healing as a Tune-Up

It is also possible to use awareness of the energy fields for energetic tune-ups. You might plan to engage in healing activities at a certain time, regardless of whether or not you feel a need right then. Or you could build energy healing into your daily meditation practice, set aside a weekly time for personal development, or book a healing like a regular monthly massage. Regular healings of this sort act like a tune-up or a check-up. With such an open-ended approach, any topic can arise and show itself to you. This gives your higher energies a good opportunity to bring your attention to something you might be overlooking. It is also a good way to find underlying issues beneath normal parts of life that may not appear problematic. Suppose for instance you go exploring and discover some unhealed energies with your mother about how you felt restricted or misunderstood as a child. These wounds may not have been serious enough to create triggering with her, but you will still feel much freer and more empowered in yourself as well as more loving with your mother after you have healed them.

There are lots of ways of exploring your energy field without any specific issue in mind. You can go into any chakra and explore what it has to show you. You could also go looking for dark energy anywhere. Or you can just skim through your current life and see what comes up. I remember a client who arrived for a healing with nothing specific on her mind. As we moved into her field she began to cry, but she didn't know why. She told me her house had been up for sale for many weeks but there had been no offers yet and she suddenly felt very sad about it all. The feeling was in her heart chakra. She moved her point of awareness down into her heart chakra and found the pattern. As she moved her point of awareness into the core of the pattern, she went back to memories of giving birth to her children in the house and how well it had supported her then. She realized she didn't want to pass the house along to someone who might not love it as well as she and her family had. So with the help of her higher energies, she thanked the house and set an intention to help find it a good new owner. That evening the family did a ritual of gratitude and said goodbye to the house; they received an offer within days. Maybe the offer would have come anyway, but maybe her attachment was blocking potential purchasers from feeling like buying. The open-ended healing opportunity led her to a more complete and happy resolution to her story.

It is also possible to engage in energetic activities that aren't related specifically to healing old wounds, but more to invigorating the energy field. This is looking after the energy field itself, like maintaining a tool. You can breathe through the chakras, breathe big love through the chakras, breathe colors into the body, connect with light of different types such as gold or platinum. You can connect with the energies of the earth and the elements to revitalize your physical and etheric body. Or you can flush higher energies through your field for clearing and cleaning. There are a wide variety of ways to make use of energy awareness to revitalize your energy field. Anything that works to bring the higher spiritual energies through your denser bodies will make you feel stronger and clearer. You can get inventive and see what works for you. The more you make a habit of caring for your energy fields, the better tuned they will be to serving you. As with exercising the physical body, energetic health will be improved by regularly maintaining the energy fields.

Physical Healing

This leads me to an obvious way to integrate energy healing skills into normal life which is in relation to physical healing. This is an area so vast that I couldn't possibly do it justice in a few short paragraphs. But the theory is the same. Everything that is in the physical body is also in the energy fields. So any time there is a disease or disorder in the physical body, it is also present in the subtle bodies. The energetic template of the disease can be seen as a pattern of energy within the body, and can be accessed by moving consciousness into the emotional, mental or soul fields there. Different diseases have different templates of energy, different consciousness, different reasons for appearing as manifest reality. Using the skills of energy healing allows us to get in beneath the usual symptom-based healing to unpack the core reasons for the illness. In Chapter 5 I showed how to use the etheric template for physical healing of an injury. The same skill can be used for healing of diseases and disorders as well.

Whenever you find yourself not feeling well, take a few moments to go within, get connected and drop down into the core of the illness. You will likely uncover a hidden truth about your current life, such as being exhausted and needing time off, or a painful situation with some person. Connecting with your higher energies and asking for guidance will often reveal a new way of getting your needs met. The illness can be a manifestation of the dilemma or issue you're facing. By bringing your awareness to the location of the disease, uncovering your own hidden feelings and beliefs and inviting your higher energies to provide new understandings, you can shift the physical dimension to a healthier state of beingness. Energy awareness and healing can be applied in all sorts of physical healing situations. I have used it in the dentist's chair while under the dreaded drill. Staying connected, asking for help, staying relaxed and otherwise occupied has helped me come successfully through what could otherwise have been unpleasant trauma. It can be used in childbirth, surgical recovery, transplant acceptance and any physical healing.

Cross-Fertilization in Healing

It is also possible and desirable to combine energy awareness and healing with almost any other healing modality. You can move your awareness within and connect with your higher energies before and during any therapeutic activity, then engage your ability to observe what's happening in your subtle fields. By combining energy awareness and healing skills with talk therapy, massage, osteopathy, acupuncture or any other healing modality, you can bring greater revelation and healing to your process. Purposely using the higher energies will help to transform issues and bring resolution and completion to any therapeutic process. There is a rich opportunity for cross-fertilization in combining methods. Anything is possible. Being connected with your own higher energies, and being willing to explore your own make-up more deeply can only lead to more powerful and profound healings.

Chapter Eleven

Putting it all Together—Spiritual Enlightenment

We have seen how it is possible to use the energy fields to live more self-realized lives and to heal old wounds and behaviors. This is useful since it helps us to become happier, more fully developed people, turning up in the world embodying more productive creativity and willing to negotiate and compromise rather than argue and defend. This is all to the good, but not the only way the energy fields can be used. I consider their ultimate use as a path to spiritual evolution and enlightenment. Evolving from the normal human condition to a more mature spirituality can happen through incorporating more and more of the consciousness of the spiritual dimensions into our daily lives. Each of the energy fields takes us a step closer to our Source. Following the fields is a path of enlightenment anyone can follow. Knowledge of the fields can be combined with any spiritual discipline or spiritual practice. Integrating the energy fields into mystical awareness enhances what is possible in human spiritual development.

Any writing about spiritual growth is linear by necessity and incapable of touching the essence of the experience. As we progress on our spiritual journeys, we dissolve, shift, morph and emerge over and over again into new states of beingness. To imagine that such a complex process could be written about in a logical fashion seems mistaken. The states of spiritual awareness are vast and varied and can only be known through being lived. Yet the process of spiritual evolution can be enhanced by integrating information about the energy fields. I offer here some basic information about the stages of enlightenment, while acknowledging that the actual experiences are transcendent beyond description and differ greatly between individuals and through time.

What I mean by enlightenment can't just happen in a moment, even if an individual has a profound mystical experience. Instead, I'm referring to a process of incorporating spiritual expansion into normal life that is necessary to becoming a spiritually evolved human. This is a tough path with many challenges. There will be break-through moments in which vast new experiences open and profound truths are revealed. These are states of wonderful spiritual awareness that give us something to aim for. But eventually we have to integrate those vast experiences with everyday life to become more spiritually mature. Old dark habits have to be cleared away to make room for more light and love. Great poetry and inspirational works have emerged from the blissful moments of God-awareness. Passionate pleas and devout intentions are written about the difficulty of staying there.

Altered states of awareness occur when a person has shifted consciousness into an expanded dimension of his or her field. This may happen intentionally through meditation or another spiritual practice, or it may happen spontaneously. In either case, the person experiences a state that reflects the nature of the dimension they're tapping into. Anything can happen in these moments of spiritual contact. The experience may be powerful or subtle, like fire, conversation or floating in the void. Spirit Guides may make themselves known, or there might be clarity about the true nature of the physical or human world. There may be visions or journeys or teachings. Anything is possible. But when the experience has passed, the person's awareness rebounds back into their denser fields and the clouds of mental illusion close over again.

At first, it is hard to stay connected with the subtle fields because the higher dimensions vibrate with unconditional love but the smaller fields don't. Spiritual breakthroughs may be profound, but the density closes in again all too quickly. We get pulled from our loving experiences back into feeling misunderstood, victimized or hopeless. Dark areas have to be cleared and the relevant beliefs transformed before the lower fields can resonate with the higher energies. Unfortunately, old thought forms don't just go away. As we explored in previous chapters, the individual has to do the inner work of finding the wounds and healing with the truth of love. Whenever an old wound gets triggered, the person exposes a dark location that isn't able to hold the love yet. The seeker may get frustrated, thinking "what's wrong with me? I experienced God yesterday, but today I'm squabbling with my family again!" Parts of the field are able to vibrate with love, while other parts aren't.

As the dark places are healed, the person radiates more light and love in the smaller fields. The field becomes less dense, more enlightened and vibrates at a higher frequency. The person becomes able to open to the higher dimensions more easily and to embody more of their loving perspective in everyday life. As time goes on, the smaller fields expand and become more enlightened, while the vaster, more powerful fields become more accessible. It is a journey of enlightenment in every sense of the word.

It's probably true that we walk the stages of enlightenment over many lifetimes, or at least that spiritual discovery is an on-going exploration of humanity. Whether this is true as individual souls or as a collective isn't clear and may not be important. What seems true though is that a level of spiritual awareness is integrated throughout our soul fields and can be accessed for continued learning. In different lives we're drawn to the mystical path, seeking to know God more deeply in our human experience. In different lives, either individually or collectively, we tackle different aspects of the journey. Some lives we cloister away, practicing deep communion with our spiritual nature and building up spiritual awareness at our soul level. Other lives we embrace daily life and challenge ourselves to bring our spiritually loving nature into the human arena. These lifetimes can be important for clearing out dark habits. In each lifetime we progress, reaching higher states of spiritual awareness. The stage of enlightenment we've attained at the end of each life is integrated in the soul field, ready to be re-initiated at another time.

Although we carry our spiritual awareness in our soul, we still have to be drawn to spiritual experience at the personality level to begin walking the path again. Sometimes it takes a wake-up call to initiate the new lifetime's searching, such as a brush with death, an accident, illness, divorce or unemployment. The shock to our habits offers an opportunity to look deeper into the purpose of our existence. Other times the call of spirit is heard from childhood. But regardless of the age at which it starts, it seems that in each lifetime the personality has to do the work of learning what the soul already knows. We begin to search for answers, to explore what else there is to life than just the physical world. This learning process continues until the information in our mental body corresponds with the experience of our souls and we catch up with ourselves. Then we begin the new work of the current incarnation. For this reason, it seems the spiritual journey goes quickly and easily at the beginning and feels like remembering things we already know but have forgotten. But as we progress further we start to slow down, reaching for new states of spiritual awareness that aren't as integrated into the soul yet. Eventually we begin to attain states of awareness that our soul has little experience of and the pace of our journey slows down again. We seem to settle into a mystical relationship with God that represents the evolution of our soul in the current lifetime.

The Evolving Mind

We humans live mostly through our minds, so it seems important to address the role of the mind in the journey of spiritual development. Let us separate the mind from its underlying consciousness for a moment to explore this inner relationship. We need our minds to be our friends on the path of enlightenment, to help us along through curiosity and a willingness to focus on the sometimes difficult tasks of spiritual evolution. After all, the personality is the vehicle for the journey of soul and spirit. Spirit can't have the human experience and the soul can't evolve without the personality doing the work. Sitting meditating in a cave might make it easy to get to God but there would be very little for the personality to do. In our modern world, the personality has to be willing to be the testing ground. Even though it is the densest field and often engages with dark consciousness, it is still in charge of the route to enlightenment.

To begin with, the mind has to be interested enough in spiritual experience to want to explore it. Then its explorations have to elicit enough meaning to develop a commitment to the path. It has to be willing to make choices and trade-offs that support the journey, even though that might entail giving up something it would actually prefer. For example, the mind might know it would enjoy watching a ball game more than meditating, but will choose to meditate anyway. But the mind can easily become a hindrance as well, getting in the way through sabotage or over-enthusiasm. It can play devil's advocate and poo-poo spiritual ideas, or play teacher's pet, saying "Oh, ask me, ask me! I'm sure I know the answer!" Eventually, on the path of enlightenment, the mind has to become willing to give up its exalted role and take a back seat to spirit. It has to learn to surrender to the higher self and act as the servant rather than the master. Throughout the processes of spiritual discovery, the mind has to be involved, but not too involved. Having a good balance between enough mind and not too much mind is an ongoing dance on the path of enlightenment.

Our minds go through their own evolution in the search for spirit. In the beginning stages of enlightenment, we become curious about what else there might be to life. The evolution begins when we ask our minds to explain God to us. This is problematic since the mind doesn't know God; all it knows is how to store memories and analyze bits of information. So to find answers to our spiritual questions, the mind works with spiritual thoughts through reading books, attending lectures or exploring ideas from other people's spiritual experiences. There's a lot of talking and thinking about the concepts, but little or no felt experience to compare it to. Sometimes in the reading or the listening there is a sudden rush of feeling, like a glimpse of another dimension. This is exciting and can lead us further along. It proves to the mind that there's something happening and the effort is worthwhile.

As we accumulate ideas and minor experiences, we usually become more interested in pursuing spiritual work. We might decide to join a group or to try meditating regularly. But if we start to have real spiritual experiences, the mind can really begin to get in the way. It can sabotage our spiritual development, especially if the experience wasn't what we 'had in mind', or if we're mistaking the voice of the dark for our own inner discernment. The spiritual experience may have seemed boring, like nothing was happening; or maybe it was too simple. If we're expecting the same intensity as the personality level, we'll be disappointed. Or the experience might have seemed frightening, out-of-control, or totally unfamiliar and incomprehensible. Or the mind might grab hold of a real experience and demolish it, saying 'It was just the light playing tricks with my eyes', or 'I must have imagined it.' Whether or not we continue on our journey and how fast we move will depend on whether or not we're willing to let the mind move to the back seat. If we still need our minds to be in control, either we'll deprive ourselves of the experience of spirit and abandon the whole venture, or we'll slow the journey down considerably.

Often the first really deep experience of spirit comes without expecting it, without the mind playing any role in setting it up. Suddenly we access an expanded state and have a profound new experience. We get a new point of reference and the mind stores a memory of a significantly different quality. At this point, the mind will probably come onside and accept that spiritual phenomena can really happen. So now we're ready to really progress in our spiritual exploration, surrendering into spiritual experience and exploring new inner territories.

Unfortunately, the mind is now likely to get involved in the process in new ways. For example, it might try to replicate the original experience by trying to remember exactly what happened. It attempts to re-create the experience through remembering and thereby gets in the way of a new experience happening. Or, as we begin to meditate regularly, the mind wants to organize all the new material. Each meditation gets stored in the mental body and the mind begins to form new beliefs about what's happening and why. If it can't prevent us from going to spirit, it can join us there. Its job is to interpret and analyze, so it gets to work interpreting and analyzing spiritual experiences. It creates a new structure of spiritual beliefs and looks for new things to attach to. It ends up thinking that if we sit in a certain position our meditation will be deeper, or if we follow a certain discipline we'll get to God faster. The mind may feel transformed beyond recognition and no longer identify as a family member or with an occupation. But instead it starts identifying as a seeker or a Buddhist or a cabalist. The mind creates a new self-identity and gets just as attached to it as it was to the original one. It creates a new spiritual ego.

All these mental systems of sabotage must be recognized and overcome before consciousness can finally start to delve into the unknowable. Eventually, the mind learns that it can trust the higher energies; that the advice and support it receives are unquestionably good. Then the mind becomes willing to surrender to the higher self and gets comfortable with not being in charge and not knowing. In fact, the mind is greatly relieved at not having to know everything and be in charge of everything. But, the more expanded the dimensions of spirit we access and the vaster and more powerful our experiences become, the more impressive we can become to our minds. Again, in order to integrate these experiences purely, the mind has to give up any attachment to having had them. The mind can take a long time before it willingly gives up spiritual materialism and spiritual status. Eventually though, the ego dissolves, and the mind fully and totally surrenders to the higher self.

Even in the very expanded states of spiritual awareness and connection, we are still human. We still have a body, a personality level and a mind. We still go about the business of our daily lives, reacting to the stimuli life brings to us. So we might ask, what is the function of the enlightened mental body? Seen in its proper perspective, this higher mind becomes a creative tool in the unfolding universe. It brings inspiration, insight and wisdom to our human experiences by being an open channel for the intelligence of the higher self. It transforms vast understandings into expressible units through language, allowing us to communicate our experience to others. It can provide stored information or historical references while living fully engaged in the moment. It helps us to send and receive love through communicating. We use it to create new ideas, inventions, art, music and all creative expressions. Through scientific inquiry, we also use it to explore and understand how life functions. The mind is here partly so we as God can know ourself through conscious thought, as well as through all our other manifestations. But the higher mind can be set aside when there is an experience that would be limited by its engagement. It has a purpose and can be used efficiently as it was intended without getting in the way of other types of experience. At this point in the evolution of consciousness, the mind has truly become the servant of the spirit.

The Energy Fields as a Map to Enlightenment

Philosophers and writers have long wondered about the nature of mystical experiences. Is there a similarity among different people's experience of the divine? Just what exactly are they tapping into? Can it be a controlled experience available to everyone, or are there 'saintly' people who are somehow blessed in a way normal mortals aren't? In energetic terms, the path of enlightenment is one of expanding consciousness into bigger and bigger dimensions of the field and learning to live through the human form from there. Everyone has the potential to become enlightened. It's part of our design. With an awareness of the human energy fields and the processes of expansion, the entire path of enlightenment becomes attainable for anyone. A person walks the path by expanding his or her awareness through the dimensions of the energy fields and integrating the awareness that comes as a result.

Let's consider a physical example to get a feel for how spiritual expansion happens. Suppose you lived in a house with a front door and three rooms. In the first room you did physical things, in the second you had emotional experiences, and in the last you did your thinking. Your entire life was enclosed within these three rooms. But one day you began to wonder if there was anything beyond these rooms. As you started to look, you realized that there was a door you hadn't noticed before. It took a little to get the door open, but beyond it there were a large number of unknown rooms, each filled with different activities and experiences. These rooms felt older and more interesting to you and less affected by your concerns about the outer world. It would take you quite some time to explore all the rooms, to find out how you felt in them and what was possible to do in them. You would still live in the original three rooms, especially as you engaged through the front door with the rest of the world, but what you thought about, how you felt and what activities you engaged in would all change as you integrated the experiences and information from the new-found rooms. It would take a while for you to fully integrate the experiences into your thoughts and feelings, and into your interactions with the world beyond.

Now suppose you had become familiar with the new rooms and began to wonder if there might be something else beyond all the rooms, so you started looking again. This time you found a hidden doorway into a beautiful landscape with extensive gardens and forests, vast and beautiful and deeply nurturing and welcoming. In the new land, the sun always shone and the air was always sweet. Again, it would take you a while to explore this new terrain. To your amazement, you would realize that there were windows in all your rooms that you had never noticed before, and the light and sweet air from the gardens could fill any of the rooms any time you opened the window. You could explore the old rooms with the new light and find dark corners you hadn't seen before. You could clean up the rooms, removing the dirt that you could now see. Again, it would take you a long time to re-explore and clean up all your rooms, integrating your new enlightened point of view into both the original three as well as into all the others and the outer world.

The spiritual journey is similar to this discovery. We live in the personality level, very busy and occupied with the three rooms of body, emotion and thought. Then we find the doorway to our soul and begin a long process of discovery and integration. There is much to explore and eventually we become familiar with what our soul has to offer. But somewhere along the way we discover there's another entire landscape beyond the personality and soul, a place of light and love and the spiritual energies of the higher self. As we explore this new place, we see all our old ways in a new light, and once again change our thoughts, feelings and behaviors. The integration process is longer now since we need to revisit and transform all the rooms of our soul and personality, but eventually we integrate the light of the higher monadic self throughout our field.

Once we're living a soul-inspired life, enlightened by our monadic energies most of the time, we may begin to perceive another door, an invisible door in the wall of the farthest garden. After knocking, we wait, sometimes for a long time until finally we are ushered through. We are met and escorted into an Ashram of a spiritual master. In the ashram we are taken in hand by a Master teacher and taught much about spiritual reality. We see that everything is made of consciousness, that time doesn't exist, and that intention and love create all realms. We see through all the illusions of human history and learn how to live from a transcendent state. We visit the ashram in meditations and nightly dreams, but aren't able to integrate the lessons into the rooms of the house yet. The information is just too radical a departure from the reality we have known and lived within.

After a long time we become ready to begin integrating the teachings into our human framework. We realize that the very air itself is directed from beyond the ashram and we see our house dissolve into a structure of conscious light. Never again do we live as we did before, believing in a separate house and a significant personal history. Eventually we become one with the masters, taking our own place as a teacher of the light in the human world. This process is akin to meeting and working with the energies in the Master level of our fields. But as Masters, we are still not fully enlightened humans. We must still find our way to the source of all life everywhere, a journey into the consciousness of the atoms and vibrations of love and light that underlie all the familiar terrains.

The Soul Merge

The first opening to spirit happens when a person opens that first door and asks the first questions about what else might exist in life. The initial question opens the personality to the possibility that there's more to life than just the physical world. This awakening brings the potential for awareness of the soul and its spiritual journey and can set the person on a path toward spiritual enlightenment. The question may happen in childhood or later. A person will be drawn to spiritual activities at different ages depending partly on what stage of spiritual enlightenment is already integrated in their soul fields and the family they're raised in. If a person hasn't awakened to the spiritual journey during youth, at some point in adulthood they're likely to wake up and begin to search for meaning in their lives. The wake-up moment begins to open the personality field to the existence of the soul level and beyond.

This first stage of spiritual development is mostly an intellectual searching process. There will be moments of experiential awakening when the person begins to 'get it', but mostly this is a mental body stage. There will be some wonderful experiences in which the person really feels the presence of soul or spirit, but these will still be few and far between. The search continues until a day comes when the individual really senses the energetic presence of his or her soul in a big way. There is a rush of feeling of revelation, an 'Ah-hah!' that makes everything in life feel different. Things start to make sense in a new way and the person feels like they've come home to themselves. The person may experience rushes of energy or uncontrollable shaking for a period of time as the soul level energies are felt and integrated into the body.

Since the personality is the densest of all the nonphysical dimensions and the emotional and mental bodies are very compelling and intense, as the person begins to integrate the presence of the soul field, there's a sense of relief. The soul feels lighter and less demanding than the personality. It still feels human, but it's more relaxed and wiser. There's a bigger picture and a longer timeline. Emotional triggers are softer and the person gets some breathing room from his or her own knee-jerk reactions. There's a more evolved understanding of human interaction and the person's own wisdom begins to overrule the wounds of their personality. They get a better perspective on what's going on around them and find forgiveness more easily. There's more love and acceptance in all aspects of their life. Since the soul has been around much longer than the personality, it's wiser and gentler. Living from the soul level makes human life a much nicer experience. In merging the soul with the personality, the soul energies flow through into daily life. In the previous chapter on self-realization we explored much of what this stage is like.

Energetically what's happening is that the personality field is transforming to be able to resonate with the soul field. Negative thoughts held in the mental body are being challenged by soul level beliefs. The soul is becoming more dominant and guiding the personality. This causes the personality to change, altering the frequency it vibrates at and raising it to a more loving vibration. As dark beliefs are replaced by loving ones, the personality field holds more light and its frequency changes. The personality field opens energetically and merges with the energies of the soul field. They flow easily and harmoniously together, still distinct, but resonating together. This process is known as the soul merge.

The Monadic Merge

In the soul merge, the personality changes to allow the soul energies to flow through to daily life. In the monadic merge, both the personality and the soul have to change to allow the energies of the monad to flow through both. The monadic merge integrates monadic energies with both the soul and the personality levels. This is a much more challenging journey than the soul merge for at least two reasons. First, it requires clearing dark from the soul level as well as the personality, and second, it puts spirit ahead of humanity as the starting point for self-identity and life-experience. Clearing dark consciousness from the soul level involves healing core beliefs and archetypal patterns from past-life experiences. It requires an absolute willingness to surrender judgments and opinions and to get ruthless about clearing out old dark beliefs. This is not an easy task in today's world. All around us we're offered opportunities to collude with dark beliefs and to stay attached to our 'issues'. Staying in the light can put us out-of-sync with the culture we live in. As well, shifting to a spirit-centered reality takes a great deal of time spent in the spiritual realms. This merge is not for occasional meditators but for those whose spiritual path is at the center of their lives.

In order for the monadic merge to be complete, the places in both the soul and personality that do not resonate in harmony with the loving spiritual consciousness of the monad have to change. This requires us to eliminate our dark concepts of humanity in others and in ourselves. It involves deep soul-searching to find all our dark beliefs that are not love-based and to transform them until we become unconditionally loving, accepting and supportive of every person and every living thing as a perfect face of God. It also requires ruthless self-scrutiny in everyday life to clear old behaviors and habits of thought that harm the self or others. Merging with monadic energies is a long and difficult stage of enlightenment because all attachments to human weaknesses have to be given up. There can be no more justifying dark responses. The person has to know the answer to the question "Am I willing to choose love every time?" Choosing love allows us to see beyond the veils of illusion to the deeper truth of reality that transcends the duality of good and bad. We continue seeking the experiences of spirit and love more and more deeply as we come to know ourselves as faces of God consciousness. We relate more and more sincerely to ourselves as Spirit having a human experience. The soul is still human-based, relating to the universe from a human perspective. But the monad is all Spirit and relates to the universe as a creative exploration of God.

Before the merge begins, we're familiar with the monadic energies as a state we experience during meditation and sometimes for periods of days. During the merging, there's a long period when we continue working to bring both the personality and the soul into alignment with the loving beliefs of the monad. This period may last for years, or possibly even lifetimes. The merge is complete when the frequencies of the personality and the soul both vibrate with the love-based frequency of the monad during daily life and normal experiences. This is also known as the ascension process. After the merge, the monadic state of awareness becomes our regular experience of living. It's like living with the peace and connectedness of a meditative state at all times. This is not to say that we never experience the darker side of life any more. Unfortunately, the temptations of the dark continue to exist, but our likelihood of choosing them diminishes toward zero. If we do choose to experience a dark aspect, we do it with full awareness that it's happening, why we are choosing to explore it, and we take full responsibility for its consequences in the web of life.

A person integrating the monadic self will be deeply committed to his or her spiritual path. They will meditate deeply and take for granted their connection with Spirit. They will likely know their guiding spirits well and have Master level energies working with them even if they don't relate to these energies as personalities. They will have found their service to humanity and likely have transformed their lives to serving their higher work. They may have left an old life behind that couldn't hold the energies of their subtle experiences. They will be pure and unconditionally loving in their relationships with other people. They will no longer believe in the illusions of their mental bodies or anyone else's. A person who is able to hold the monadic energies and work with them in regular life is truly living in 'heaven on earth'. They're able to know themselves and everyone else on all levels as divine beings of love. They will have transcended the limitations of their human experiences and live with delight and fulfillment, even when things aren't going well in their lives. They will have awe and reverence for the fantastic invention of their humanity and live with acceptance of all the conditions of their lives. And they will still be human, fully experiencing the emotions and thoughts of their human beingness. They will still have stories and challenges in their everyday lives. It is in how they meet these challenges that the integrating of the monadic energies becomes finalized.

It is a very long process to integrate the energies of the monadic levels into human life. There is so much old darkness on the soul levels and in our collective spiritual history that we can't just go around or leapfrog over. There's no way to grow more enlightened without doing the work of enlightening the dark places, no matter which field we're engaging with. Healing of the soul level is a long process, but very worthwhile. The ascension process is accomplished when the personality and the soul have expanded and become fully integrated with the Monad. The person can shift his or her consciousness back and forth between the three fields easily as they are all open and resonating harmoniously. The frequency of the smaller fields has increased to the point where they vibrate with the love of the monadic field. After this is complete, the Monad becomes the equivalent of the personality, and the individual lives from their higher energies all the time.

The Higher Merges

Attempting to describe the stages of enlightenment that involve the higher dimensions is not easy to do in words since the experiences are so far beyond the conceptual basis in which words are founded. What can be said is that the same process seems to be repeated, but at the next level out. It seems that merging into full Master consciousness takes clearing all darkness from the monadic level in all concurrent lives the monad is responsible for. This requires a commitment to spirit and divine service that transcends anything that can be spoken of in human terms. Embodying these higher aspects of consciousness begins to warp the fabric of reality as we know it. Consciousness is not always the same as our human self experiences it. We meet and know aspects of our spirit selves that have nothing to do with our earthly experiences. Reality changes. Eventually we're able to stay open to the unified field of God consciousness while still being embodied in the physical dimension because all our fields are suffused with the divine reality of humanity. Integrating the Master level energies with the soul and personality cause complete changes in the way we engage with the world around us. We absolutely can't not do the spiritual work we are called to. It becomes the sole purpose of continuing our human existence.

To begin to carry the frequencies of the Master and co-creative dimensions, we have to say no to all dark at the monadic level, regardless of what lifetime or life-form it's in. We recognize a vast, inter-temporal gestalt of Self that we experience from our human perspective. Making a choice to eradicate all dark from all definitions of this Self causes ripples of change to move out through time and space. This is a major testing point in our spiritual evolution. At the Master level, there is no negativity per se. The duality of light and dark is transcended. However, there can still be darkness within the human experience of Mastery because of the temptations posed to the spirit while in human form. It takes great wisdom, purity and commitment to love to stay clear of the seductions of human life. If the personality succumbs to the seductions, the resulting dark energies will have to be cleared before the person will be free to do their big work again. Once they have purified the negative consequences, they will be able to channel the Master energies again. The human soul will also be living through these experiences and learning how to carry such massive spiritual energy. The likelihood of succumbing to the temptations again diminishes and the soul's ability to carry out the Master level work on the planet increases.

Practical Exercises

- *Assuming Beliefs are not True*

I have a basic rule for myself. Whenever I discover that I believe something is true, I then assume my belief is wrong, that I don't know what is true, and that life will reveal itself. Instead of believing my beliefs, I disbelieve them. I don't automatically assume that the opposite is true, since that would be another belief. Instead I assume that I don't know what is true. Then I watch to see what will be revealed to me. In this way I stay in more intimate contact with the unfolding world around me. Some beliefs are worth keeping because they make life run according to our collective rules. You do want to keep driving on the correct side of the road and turning up at work on the appropriate days. But recognizing the belief as a social convention is different from holding fast to it as a necessary belief. You can try challenging all your beliefs and see what happens.

- *What did I learn today?*

Here's a wonderful exercise I learned from Tom Brown Jr. Keep a separate journal by your bed and every night take a moment to reflect on the question "What did I learn today?" Record as much as you can. You'll begin to track changes in your experiences, your flowing growth and new insights. Over time, you'll capture a great amount of wisdom that passes fleeting by in each day. Eventually you don't need to keep recording it. The idea is only partly to keep track of the information. Moreso, the idea is to come into relationship with yourself as an ever-changing stream of consciousness that grows and changes and adapts daily. If you allow your beliefs to change, you can learn new ways of being that work better for you and bring more peace and happiness into your life.

- *Dissolving Identity*

Here is one of my favorite meditations. It is one of the ways I dissolve most thoroughly into the mystery. Sit quietly and bring your awareness inside, disconnecting from the mental body. Now feel from the inside what you identify yourself with. Suppose you say 'I am my body'. Then feel the part of yourself that is your body and rest for a moment in the experience of being your body. Then move behind that place. Take your consciousness deeper, shifting to a place behind the first one, from which you can honestly feel the truth that 'I am not my body'. Feel what it feels like to be not your body. Now notice what comes up next that you feel you are. Maybe the next statement will be 'I am a parent.' Do the same thing, first feeling the self that is the parent, then moving behind it to a place where you are not that. As you drop into that deeper layer of consciousness, you will feel the earlier step dissolve away. Keep going, and it won't be long before you know you are God. But watch out for what the mental body will do with that. Make the statement 'I am not my idea of God' and see what happens.

- *Exploring the Higher Chakras*

To begin to explore the higher chakras, follow the same process you developed in the earlier chapters. Begin by moving your point of awareness in from your third eye and then move up into your crown chakra. You can then climb gradually out, one chakra at a time, fully experiencing each as you go. The seventh, eighth and ninth are the soul level; the tenth, eleventh and twelfth are the monadic level; the thirteenth, fourteenth and fifteenth are the Master level and so on. In the extroverted, relational chakras of eight, eleven and fourteen, you might have a sense of guiding energies or of community. In the introverted ninth, twelfth and fifteenth you may feel more a sense of your own soul and higher self. Each time you visit a dimension you will have a similar but different experience. In general I recommend waiting to engage with the master level and beyond until after you have become quite familiar with life at the monadic level.

Or, you could move up through the crown by full dimension, intending to go to the soul, then the monad. Again, the experiences will be quite different and will offer insights to different aspects of your life. I recommend that you keep track of it somehow, through journaling or art work. While it is important not to let the mind demolish the experiences through over-analysis, it is still a worthwhile intention to grow and develop through the experiences. Often there is a lot of guidance or insights given and keeping track of them helps the mind to learn from them.

Once you get the hang of connecting with your higher self, you can do it anywhere, anytime. By connecting first thing in the morning, last thing at night and at any moment throughout the day, you begin to really experience your life through the higher fields. The wisdom, love and guidance are perpetually available and they begin to feel totally natural. As you begin to live from the whole you, you get to choose your responses and reactions to the world you inhabit.

Living from an aware personality, you can pay attention to your emotions for feedback about what works for you; or watch your thought patterns to increase your potential options. You can relax your need to know or to be right about things, and not jump to your mental body to explain the world to you. You can always access your higher dimensions to perceive a bigger, loving view of whatever is going on. You can observe when something affects you negatively and bring wisdom and love to resolving it. You can make use of your own spiritual nature to inspire, guide and ultimately inhabit your life. You can eliminate dark concepts and choose love more and more often. You can heal and transform until you glow with the inner radiance of your own unique, divine nature. Eventually you can turn up fully engaged in the creative processes of your existence, fully inhabiting your unique and perfect place in the universe. Imagine a world in which we all know all we're made of, where we easily choose love as the basis for all our interactions. This world is right here, inside our own energy fields, just waiting to be discovered.

Endnotes

1. Tom Brown Jr's The Tracker School: Tracking, Nature and Wilderness Survival, PO Box 173, Asbury, N.J., 08802 or www.trackerschool.com.

2. The former School of Energy Mastery became The Jaffe Institute and has now evolved into The University of Spiritual Healing and Sufism. It is located in northern California and can be contacted through its administrative offices at PO Box 91744, Austin, TX, 78709 or www.sufiuniversity.org.

3. For those of you who are interested in astrology, my birth data is September 19, 1953; 3:42 am; Kitchener, Ontario, Canada. Pluto and Venus are conjunct each other and the ascendant in the first house in Leo. Mars is also in the first house but in Virgo. In the third house in Libra is Mercury as well as Neptune conjunct Saturn. And in the sixth house in Aquarius is the moon conjunct North node. Together, these configurations seem to help me perceive and communicate about the subtle energy fields in my work as a healer and teacher.

4. "The universe is only 4 percent ordinary matter, the stuff of stars and trees and people," quoted from Charles Seife, "Illuminating the Dark Universe", *Science*, vol. 302, no. 5653, 2003, pp. 2038–9.

5. Stalking Wolf, quoted in Philosophy courses at The Tracker School by Tom Brown Jr., December, 1995, New Jersey.

6. "Over 95 percent of DNA has a largely unknown function", quoted from Jaan Suurkula, M.D., "Junk DNA", *The Gene Exchange*, no 2, 1996.

7. For example, see Andy Coghlin, "'Junk' DNA makes compulsive reading", issue 2608 *New Scientist*, 13 June 2007, page 20; F. Flam, "Hints of

a language in junk DNA", *Science* vol. 266, no. 1320, 1994; Aria Pearson, "Genomics: Junking the Junk DNA", *New Scientist*, 11 July 2007, issue 2612; or "Exploring 'Junk DNA' In The Genome", *Science Daily*, June 16, 2007, Lawrence Berkeley National Laboratory.

8   Peter Russell, "The Primacy of Consciousness" in *Science and the Reenchantment of the Cosmos: The Rise of the Integral Vision of Reality*, Ervin Laszlo, Rochester, Vt.: Inner Traditions, 2006. See also http://www.peterrussell.com/SP/PrimConsc.php

9   "To die with dignity was a form of resistance," quoted from Martin Gilbert, *The Holocaust: The Jewish Tragedy*, London: St. Edmundsbury Press 1986. See also *Jewish Resistance: A Working Bibliography*, The Miles Lerman Center for the Study of Jewish Resistance, Center for Advanced Holocaust Studies, US Holocaust Memorial Museum; or Yehuda Bauer, "Forms of Jewish Resistance During the Holocaust," in *The Nazi Holocaust: Historical Articles on the Destruction of European Jews*. Vol. 7: *Jewish Resistance to the Holocaust*, edited by Michael R. Marrus, pp. 34–48. Westport, CT: Meckler, 1989.

10 Gary Larson, August 19, 1982, *The Complete Far Side*, vol. 1 (1980–1986), p 234, Kansas City: Andrew McMeel Publishing, 2003.

11 For a current example, see http://edition.cnn.com/2003/WORLD/asiapcf/south/ 11/26/offbeat.india.fast/index.html

"This 76-year-old Indian mystic claims to have survived the past 68 years—yes, *years*—without eating, drinking or going to the toilet. Prahlad Jani says his fasting ability is divinely inspired."
CNN.com International, Thursday, November 27, 2003,

12 "For example, 'an etheric leaf', which can be captured by Kirlian photography, provides the blueprint for the actual leaf as it develops each spring. If you mark the branch of that leaf and save the leaf, you will discover that an identical one will appear each year. The physical etheric leaf holds its pattern." Quoted from Peter Tadd, "Flowers—The Essence of Consciousness", *Positive Health*, Positive Health Publications Ltd., Portsmouth, U.K.: issue 66, July 2001. Also at http://www.positivehealth.com/article-view.php?articleid=663

13 "In the United States, about 10 to 25 percent of the recognized pregnancies and up to 75 percent of the unrecognized pregnancies end in miscarriages every year, most during the first 13 weeks of pregnancy, according to the American College of Obstetricians and Gynecologists," quoted from *Nubella News*, "Improving Your Odds for a Healthy Pregnancy", May 2002, the American College of Obstetricians and Gynecologists.

14 Susan L. Farber, *Identical Twins Reared Apart*, New York: Basic Books, 1981

15 See for example, Language of Light, Spiritual School of Ascension, www.calltoascend.org.

16 J. J. Hurtak, *The Book of Knowledge: The Keys of Enoch*, Los Gatos, California: The Academy for Future Science, 1977

17 J. R. R. Tolkein, *The Lord of the Rings*, London: George Allen & Unwin, 1954, 1955

978-0-595-45940-7
0-595-45940-4

Printed in the United States
140511LV00001B/10/P